Goodbye To All That

ROBERT GRAVES

CASSELL · LONDON

CASSELL & COMPANY LTD
35 Red Lion Square, London wc1
Melbourne, Sydney, Toronto
Johannesburg, Cape Town, Auckland

Copyright Robert Graves, 1929 and 1957
This abridged edition © Robert Graves 1966
First published 1929
This edition first published 1966

Set in 11 on 12 pt. Fournier type and printed in Great Britain
by Cox & Wyman, Ltd., London, Fakenham and Reading
F 666

CONTENTS

I

My height is given as six feet two inches, my eyes as grey, and my hair as black. To 'black' should be added 'thick and curly'. I am untruthfully described as having no special peculiarity. For a start, there is my big, once aquiline nose, which I broke at Charterhouse while foolishly playing rugger with soccer players. (I broke another player's nose myself in the same game.) That unsteadied it, and boxing sent it askew. Finally, it was operated on by an unskilful army surgeon, and no longer serves as a vertical line of demarcation between the left and right sides of my face. My mouth is what is known as 'full', and my smile is tight-lipped: when I was thirteen I broke two front teeth and became sensitive about showing them. My hands and feet are large. I weigh about twelve stone four. One shoulder is distinctly lower than the other, because of a lung wound. I do not carry a watch because I always magnetize the main-spring; during the war when an order went out that officers should carry watches and synchronize them daily, I had to buy two new ones every month. Medically, I am a good life.

My passport gives my nationality as 'British subject'. My mother's father's family, the von Rankes, were Saxon country pastors, not anciently noble. Leopold von Ranke, the first modern historian, my great-uncle, introduced the 'von'. To

Heinrich von Ranke, my grandfather, I owe my clumsy largeness, my endurance, energy, seriousness, and my thick hair. He was rebellious and even atheistic in his youth. In 1854, he went to the Crimea with the British Army as a regimental surgeon. He married, in London, my grandmother, a tiny, saintly, frightened Schleswig-Dane, daughter of Tiarks, the Greenwich astronomer. My gentler characteristics trace back to my grandmother. She had ten children; the eldest of these, my mother, was born in London. My grandfather's atheism and radicalism sobered down. He eventually returned to Germany, where he became a well-known children's doctor at Munich, and about the first in Europe to insist on clean milk for his child patients. Finding that he could not get clean milk to the hospitals by ordinary means, he started a model dairy-farm himself.

I admire my German relatives; they have high principles, are easy, generous, and serious. The men have fought duels not for cheap personal honour, but in the public interest—called out, for example, because they have protested against the scandalous behaviour of some superior officer or official. One of them lost seniority in the German consulate service because he refused to use the consulate in London as a clearing-house for secret service reports. They are not heavy drinkers either. My grandfather, as a student at the regular university 'drunks', had a habit of pouring superfluous beer into his eighteen-fortyish riding-boots, when nobody was watching. He brought up his children to speak English at home, and always looked to England as the centre of culture and progress. The women were noble and patient, and used to keep their eyes on the ground when out walking.

At the age of eighteen, my mother went to England as companion to Miss Britain, a lonely old woman who had befriended my grandmother as an orphan, and waited hand and foot on her for seventeen years. When she finally died, under the senile impression that my mother, her sole heiress, would benefit hardly at all from the will, it turned out that she had been worth £100,000. Characteristically, my mother divided the inheritance among her four younger sisters, keeping only a fifth share.

My father's family, the Graves's, have a pedigree that goes back to a French knight who landed with Henry VII at Milford Haven in 1485. They went to Dublin around 1575 and Cloghan Castle, Meath, later became their seat. My father met my mother some time in the early nineties. He had previously married one of the Irish Coopers, of Cooper's Hill, near Limerick. The Coopers were an even more Irish family than the Graves's. The story goes that when Cromwell came to Ireland and ravaged the country, Moira O'Brien, the last surviving member of the great clan O'Brien, who were the paramount chiefs of the country around Limerick, came to him one day and said, 'General, you have killed my father and my uncles, my husband and my brothers. I am left as the sole heiress of these lands. Do you intend to confiscate them?' Cromwell is said to have been struck by her magnificent presence, and to have answered that this certainly had been his intention. But that she could keep her lands, or a part of them, on condition that she married one of his officers, Ensign Cooper, whom later she ungratefully kicked to death. Jane Cooper, whom my father married, died of consumption.

My father was a poet and I am delighted when I meet people who know of him and not me. I sing some of his songs while washing up after meals, or shelling peas, or on similar occasions. He never once tried to teach me how to write, or showed any understanding of my serious poetry; being always more ready to ask advice about his own. Nor did he ever try to stop me writing. His light-hearted early work is the best. After marrying my mother and turning teetotaller, he is said to have lost something of his playfulness.

I can admire my father and mother: my father for his simplicity and persistence, and my mother for her seriousness and strength. Both for their generosity. They never bullied me, and were grieved rather than angered by my default from formal religion. In physique and general characteristics my mother's side is, on the whole, stronger in me. But I have many habits of speech and movement peculiar to the Graves's, most of them eccentric. Such as finding it difficult to walk straight down a street; fidgeting with bits of bread at table; getting tired of sentences when half-way through and leaving them in the air; walking with the hands folded in a particular way behind the back; and being subject to sudden and most disconcerting spells of complete amnesia. The most useful and, at the same time, most dangerous gift that I owe to my father's side of the family is that I am always able, when dealing with officials, or getting privileges from public institutions which grudge them, to masquerade as a gentleman. I paid so heavily for the fourteen years of my gentleman's education that I feel entitled, now and then, to get some sort of return.

2

MY father being a very busy man, an inspector of schools for the Southwark district of London, we children saw practically nothing of him except during the holidays. He occasionally played games with us, but for the most part, when not busy with educational work, was writing verse, or being president of literary or temperance societies. My mother, kept busy running the household and conscientiously carrying out her social obligations as my father's wife, did not see so much of us as she would have liked, except on Sundays or when we happened to be ill. We had a nurse, and one another, and found that companionship sufficient. My father's chief part in our education was to insist on our speaking grammatically, pronouncing words correctly, and using no slang. He left our religious instruction entirely to my mother, though he officiated at family prayers, which the servants were expected to attend, every morning before breakfast. Light punishments, such as being sent to bed early or being stood in a corner, were in the hands of my mother; the infliction of corporal punishment, never severe and given with a slipper, she reserved for my father. We learned to be strong moralists, and spent much of our time on self-examination and good resolutions. My sister Rosaleen put up a printed notice in her corner of the nursery—it might just as well have been put up by me: 'I must not say "bang bust" or "pig bucket", for it is rude.'

We were given very little pocket-money—a penny a week with a rise to twopence at the age of twelve or so—and encouraged to give part at least of any odd money that came to us from uncles or other visitors to Dr Barnardo's Homes, and to beggars. A blind beggar used to sit on the Wimbledon Hill pavement, reading the Bible aloud in Braille; he was not really blind, but could turn up his eyes and keep the pupils concealed for minutes at a time under drooping lids, which were artificially inflamed. We often gave to him. He died a rich man, and had been able to provide his son with a college education.

I went to several preparatory schools, beginning at the age of six. The very first was a dame's school at Wimbledon, but my father, as an educational expert, would not let me stay there long. He found me crying one day at the difficulty of the twenty-three-times table, and disapproved of a Question and Answer history book that we used, which began:

Question: Why were the Britons so called?

Answer: Because they painted themselves blue.

My father sent me to King's College School, Wimbledon. I was just seven years old, the youngest boy there, and they went up to nineteen. My father took me away after a couple of terms because he heard me using naughty words, and because I did not understand the lessons. I had started Latin, but nobody explained what 'Latin' meant; its declensions and conjugations were pure incantations to me. For that matter, so were the strings of naughty words. And I felt oppressed by the huge hall, the enormous boys, the frightening rowdiness of the corridors, and compulsory Rugby football of which nobody told me the rules. From there I went to Rokeby, a preparatory school of the ordinary type, also at Wimbledon, where I stayed for about three years. Here I began playing games seriously, grew quarrelsome, boastful,

6

and domineering, won prizes, and collected things. The main difference between myself and the other boys was that I collected coins instead of stamps. The value of coins seemed less fictitious to me. The headmaster caned me only once: for forgetting to bring my gym-shoes to school, and then gave me no more than two strokes on the hand. Yet even now the memory makes me hot with resentment. My serious training as a gentleman began here.

I seem to have left out one school—Penrallt, right away in the hills behind Llanbedr. I had never been away from home before. I went there just for a term, for my health. Here I had my first beating. The headmaster, a parson, caned me on the bottom because I learned the wrong prayer one Sunday by mistake. I had never before come upon forcible training in religion. At my dame's school we learned prayers too, but were not punished for mistakes; we competed for prizes— ornamental texts to take home and hang over our beds. A boy at Penrallt called Ronny was the greatest hero I had ever met. He had a house at the top of a pine-tree which nobody else could climb, and a huge knife, made from the tip of a scythe which he had stolen; and he killed pigeons with a catapult, cooked them and ate them in the tree-house. Ronny treated me very kindly; he went into the Navy afterwards, deserted on his first voyage and, we were told, was never heard of again.

I left day-school at Wimbledon because my father decided that the standard of work was not high enough to get me a scholarship at a public school. He sent me to another pre-paratory school at Rugby, where the headmaster's wife happened to be a sister of an old literary friend of his. I did not like the place. There was a secret about the headmaster which some of the elder boys shared—a somehow sinister secret. Nobody ever let me into it, but he came weeping into the class-room one day, beating his head with his fists, and groaning: 'Would to God I hadn't done it! Would to God I

7

hadn't done it!' My father took me away suddenly, a week later. The headmaster, having been given twenty-four hours to leave the country, was succeeded by the second master—a good man, who had taught me how to write English by eliminating all phrases that could be done without, and using verbs and nouns instead of adjectives and adverbs wherever possible. And when to start new paragraphs, and the difference between 'O' and 'Oh'. Mr Lush was a very heavy man, who used to stand at his desk and lean on his thumbs until they bent at right angles. A fortnight after taking over the school he fell out of a train on his head, and that was the end of him; but the school seems to be still in being. I am occasionally asked to subscribe to Old Boys' funds for memorial windows and miniature rifle ranges and so on.

I first learned rugger here. What surprised me most at this school was when a boy of about twelve, whose father and mother were in India, heard by cable that they had both suddenly died of cholera. We all watched him sympathetically for weeks after, expecting him to die of grief, or turn black in the face, or do something to match the occasion. Yet he seemed entirely unmoved, and because nobody dared discuss the tragedy with him he seemed oblivious of it—playing about and ragging just as he had done before. We found that rather monstrous. But he had not seen his parents for two years; and preparatory schoolboys live in a world completely dissociated from home life. They have a different vocabulary, a different moral system, even different voices. On their return to school from the holidays the change-over from home-self to school-self is almost instantaneous, whereas the reverse process takes a fortnight at least. A preparatory schoolboy, when caught off his guard, will call his mother 'Please matron', and always addresses any male relative or friend of the family as 'Sir', like a master. I used to do it. School life becomes the reality, and home life the illusion. In England, parents of the governing classes virtually lose all

8

intimate touch with their children from about the age of eight, and any attempts on their parts to insinuate home feeling into school life are resented.

Next, I went to Copthorne, a typically good school in Sussex. There I learned to keep a straight bat at cricket, and to have a high moral sense. They put me into the top class, and I got a scholarship—in fact I got the first scholarship of the year. At Charterhouse.

3

My mother took us abroad to stay at my grandfather's house in Germany five times between my second and twelfth year. Then he died, and we never went again. He owned a big old manor-house at Deisenhofen, ten miles from Munich; by name 'Laufzorn', which means 'Begone, anger!' Our summers there were easily the best things of my early childhood. Pine forests and hot sun, red deer, black and red squirrels, acres of blueberries and wild strawberries; nine or ten different kinds of edible mushrooms which we went into the forest to pick, and unfamiliar flowers in the fields; a farm with all the usual animals except sheep; drives through the countryside in a brake behind my grandfather's greys; and bathing in the Isar under a waterfall. The Isar was bright green, and said to be the fastest river of Europe. We used to visit the uncles who kept a peacock farm a few miles away; and a grand-uncle, Johannes von Ranke, the ethnologist, who lived on the lakeshore of Tegernsee, where everyone had buttercup-blonde hair; and occasionally my Aunt Agnes, Freifrau Baronin von Aufsess of Aufsess Castle, some hours away by train, high up in the Bavarian Alps.

Aufsess, built in the ninth century, stood so remote that it had never been sacked, but remained Aufsess property ever since. To the original building, a keep with only a ladderentrance half-way up, a medieval castle had been added. Its treasures of plate and armour were amazing. My Uncle Siegfried showed us children the chapel: its walls hung with enamelled shields of each Aufsess baron, impaled with the arms of the noble family into which he had married. He pointed to a stone in the floor which pulled up by a ring, and said: 'That is the family vault where all Aufsesses go when they die. I'll be down there one day.' He scowled comically. (But he got killed in the war as an officer of the Imperial German Staff and, I believe, they never found his body.) Uncle Siegfried had a peculiar sense of humour. One day we children saw him on the garden path, eating pebbles. He told us to go away, but of course we stayed, sat down, and tried to eat pebbles too; only to be told very seriously that children should not eat pebbles: we would break our teeth. We agreed, after trying one or two; so he chose each a pebble which looked just like all the rest, but which crushed easily and had a chocolate centre. This was on condition that we went away and left him to his picking and crunching. When we returned, later in the day, we searched and searched, but found only the ordinary hard pebbles. He never once let us down in a joke.

Among the castle treasures were a baby's lace cap that had taken two years to make; and a wine glass which my uncle's old father had noticed in the Franco–Prussian War standing upright in the middle of the square in an entirely ruined French village. For dinner, when we went there, we ate some enormous trout. My father, a practised fisherman, asked my uncle in astonishment where they came from. He explained that an underground river welled up close to the castle, and the fish which emerged with it were quite white from the darkness, of extraordinary size, and stone-blind.

They also gave us jam made of wild rose-berries, which they called 'Hetchi-Petch', and showed us an iron chest in a small, thick-walled, white-washed room at the top of the keep—a tremendous chest, twice the size of the door, and obviously made inside the room, which had no windows except arrow-slits. It had two keys, and must have been twelfth- or thirteenth-century work. Tradition ruled that it should never be opened, unless the castle stood in the most extreme danger. The baron held one key; his steward, the other. The chest could be opened only by using both keys, and nobody knew what lay inside; it was even considered unlucky to speculate. Of course, we speculated. It might be gold; more likely a store of corn in sealed jars; or even some sort of weapon—Greek fire, perhaps. From what I know of the Aufsesses and their stewards, it is inconceivable that the chest ever got the better of their curiosity. A ghost walked the castle, the ghost of a former baron known as the 'Red Knight'; his terrifying portrait hung half-way up the turret staircase which led to our bedrooms. We slept on feather beds for the first time in our lives.

Laufzorn, which my grandfather had bought and restored from a ruinous condition, could not compare in tradition with Aufsess, though it had for a time been a shooting lodge of the Bavarian kings. Still, two ghosts went with the place; the farm labourers used to see them frequently. One of them was a carriage which drove furiously along without horses and, before the days of motor cars, horrible enough. Not having visited the banqueting hall since childhood, I find it difficult to recall its true dimensions. It seemed as big as a cathedral, with stained-glass armorial windows, and bare floorboards furnished only at the four corners with small islands of tables and chairs; swallows had built rows of nests all along the sides of the ceiling. The bottom storey formed part of the farm. A carriage-drive ran right through it, with a wide, covered courtyard in the centre, where cattle were once driven to safety in times of baronial feud. On one side of the drive lay the estate steward's quarters, on the other the farm servants' inn and kitchen. In the middle storey lived my grandfather and his family. The top storey was a store for corn, apples, and other farm produce; and up here my cousin Wilhelm—later shot down in an air battle by a school-fellow of mine—used to lie for hours picking off mice with an air-gun.

Beyond the farm buildings at Laufzorn lay a large pond, fringed with irises and full of carp; my uncles netted it every three or four years. Once we watched the fun, and shouted when we saw the net pulled closer and closer to the shallow landing corner. It bulged with wriggling carp, and a big pike threshed about among them. I waded in to help, and came out with six leeches, like black rubber tubes, fastened to my legs; salt had to be put on their tails before they would leave go. The farm labourers grew wildly excited; one of them gutted a fish with his thumb, and ate it raw. I also remember the truck line between the railway station, two miles away, and the brick yard. Since the land had a fall of perhaps one in a hundred between the factory and the station, the Italians used to load their trucks with bricks; then a squad of them would give the trucks a hard shove and run along the line pushing for twenty or thirty yards; after which the trucks sailed off all by themselves towards the station.

We were allowed to climb up into the rafters of the big hay barn, and jump down into the springy hay; we gradually increased the height of the jumps. It was exciting to feel our insides left behind us in the air. Once we visited the Laufzorn cellar, not the ordinary beer cellar, but another into which we descended from the courtyard—quite dark except for a little slit window. A huge heap of potatoes lay on the floor; to get to the light, they had put out a twisted mass of long white feelers. In one corner was a dark hole closed by a gate: a secret passage from the house to a ruined monastery, a mile away— so we were told. My uncles had once been down some distance, but the air got bad and they came back; the gate had been put up to prevent anyone else trying it and never returning.

When we drove out beside my grandfather, he was acclaimed with 'Grüss Gott, Herr Professor!' by the principal personages of each village we went through. It always had a big inn with a rumbling skittle-alley, and a tall Maypole, banded like a barber's pole with blue and white, the Bavarian national colours. Apple- and pear-trees lined every road. The idea of these unguarded public fruit-trees astonished us. We could not understand why any fruit remained on them. On Wimbledon Common even the horse-chestnut-trees were pelted with sticks and stones, long before the chestnuts ripened, and in defiance of an energetic common-keeper.

Munich we found sinister—disgusting fumes of beer and cigar smoke, and intense sounds of eating in the restaurants; the hotly dressed, enormously stout population in trams and trains; the ferocious officials. Then the terrifying Morgue, which children were not allowed to visit. Any notable who died was taken to the Morgue, they told us, and put in a chair, to sit in state for a day or two. If a general, he had his uniform on; or if a burgomaster's wife, she had on her silks and jewels. Strings were tied to their fingers, and the slightest movement of a single string would ring a great bell, in case any life remained in the corpse after all. I have never verified the truth of this, but it was true enough to me. When my grandfather died, about a year after our last visit, I pictured him in the Morgue with his bushy white hair, his morning coat, his striped trousers, his decorations, and his stethoscope. And perhaps, I thought, a silk hat, gloves, and cane on a table beside him. Trying, in a nightmare, to be alive; but knowing himself dead.

The headmaster of Rokeby school who caned me for forgetting my gymnastic shoes loved German culture, and impressed this feeling on the school, so that it stood to my credit that I could speak German and had visited Germany. At my other preparatory schools this German connexion seemed something at least excusable, and perhaps even interesting. Only at Charterhouse did it rank as a social offence. My history from the age of fourteen, when I went to Charterhouse, until just before the end of the war, when I began to think for myself, is a forced rejection of the German in me. I used to insist indignantly on being Irish, and took my self-protective stand on the technical point that the father's nationality alone counted.

4

FROM my first moment at Charterhouse I suffered an oppression of spirit that I hesitate to recall in its full intensity. Something like being in that chilly cellar at Laufzorn among the potatoes, but a potato out of a different sack from the rest. The school consisted of about six hundred boys, whose chief interests were games and friendships. Everyone despised school-work; the scholars were not concentrated in a single dormitory house as at Winchester or Eton, but divided among ten, and known as 'pro's'. Unless good at games, and able to pretend that they hated work even more than the non-scholars, and ready whenever called on to help these with their work, they always had a bad time. I happened to be a scholar who really liked work, and the apathy of the class-rooms surprised and disappointed me. My first term, I was left alone more or less, it being a rule that new boys should be neither encouraged nor baited. The other boys seldom addressed me except to send me on errands, or coldly point out breaches of school convention.

In my second term the trouble began. A number of things naturally made for my unpopularity. Besides being a scholar and not outstandingly good at games, I was always short of pocket-money. Since I could not conform to the social custom of treating my contemporaries to tuck at the school shop, I could not accept their treating. My clothes, though conforming outwardly to the school pattern, were ready-made and not of the best-quality cloth that all the other boys wore. Even so, I had not been taught how to make the best of them. Neither my mother nor my father had any regard for the niceties of dress, and my elder brothers were abroad by this time. Nearly all the other boys in my house, except for five scholars, were the sons of businessmen: a class of whose interests and prejudices I knew nothing, having hitherto met only boys of the professional class. Also I talked too much for their liking. I wanted to run away.

The most unfortunate disability of all was that my name appeared on the school list as 'R. von R. Graves'. I had hitherto believed my second name to be 'Ranke'; the 'von', encountered on my birth certificate, disconcerted me. The other boys behaved secretively about their second names; and usually managed to conceal fancy ones. I could no doubt have passed off 'Ranke', without the 'von' as monosyllabic and English, but 'von Ranke' was glaring. Businessmen's sons, at this time, used to discuss hotly the threat, and even the necessity, of a trade war with the Reich. 'German' meant 'dirty German'. It meant: 'cheap, shoddy goods competing with our sterling industries'. It also meant military menace, Prussianism, useless philosophy, tedious scholarship, music-loving and sabre-rattling. Another boy in my house with a German name, though English by birth and upbringing, got much the same treatment as I did. On the other hand, a French boy in the house became very popular, though poor at games; King Edward VII had done his *entente cordiale* work thoroughly.

Of course, I always claimed to be Irish, but an Irish boy who had been in the house about a year and a half longer than myself resented this claim. He went out of his way to hurt me by physical acts of spite, like throwing ink over my school-books, hiding my games-clothes, attacking me

17

suddenly from behind corners, and by pouring water over my bed at night. I came near a nervous breakdown. School ethics prevented me from informing the housemaster of my troubles. The house-monitors, though supposed to keep order and preserve the moral tone of the house, never interfered in any case of bullying among the juniors. I tried violent resistance, but as the odds were always heavily against me this merely encouraged the ragging. Complete passive resistance would probably have been wiser.

Half-way through my second year I wrote to tell my parents that they must take me away, because I could not stand life at Charterhouse any longer: the house had made it plain that I did not belong, and was not wanted. I gave them details, in confidence, to make them take my demand seriously; but they failed to respect this confidence, believing that their religious duty would be to inform the housemaster of all I had written them. Nor did they even warn me what they were doing; but contented themselves with visiting me and preaching the power of prayer and faith. I must endure all, they said, for the sake of . . . I have forgotten what exactly—perhaps my career. The housemaster made a speech that night, after prayers, deterrent of bullying in general. He told us that he had just received a complaint from a boy's parents; making it plain at the same time how much he disliked informers and outside interference in affairs of the house. My name did not come up, but the visit of my parents on a non-holiday had excited comment. I was obliged to stay on, and be treated as an informer. Being now in the upper school, I had a study of my own. But studies could not be locked, and mine was always being wrecked. I could no longer use the ordinary house changing-room, so removed my games-clothes to a disused shower-bath. Then my heart went wrong, and the school doctor decided that I must play no more football. My last resource, to sham insanity, succeeded unexpectedly well. Soon nobody troubled except to avoid any contact with me. I got the idea from *The Book of Kings*, where David had 'scrabbled on the prison wall'.

This is not to charge my parents with treachery. Their honour is beyond reproach. Next term, I went to Charterhouse by the special train, but arrived at Waterloo too late to take a ticket; I just managed to get into a compartment before the train started. The railway company not having provided enough coaches, I had to stand all the way. At Godalming station, the crowd of boys rushing out into the station yard to secure taxis swept me past the ticket collectors, so I got a very uncomfortable ride free. I mentioned this in my next letter home, just for something to say, and my father wrote to reproach me. He said that he had himself made a special visit to Waterloo station, bought a ticket to Godalming, and torn it up . . . My mother could be even more scrupulous. A young couple on their honeymoon once stopped the night with us at Wimbledon, and left behind a packet of sandwiches, two already half-eaten. My mother sent them on.

Thrown entirely on myself, I began to write poems; which the house considered stronger proof of insanity than the formal straws I wore in my hair. On the strength of a poem I had sent to the school magazine, *The Carthusian*, I was invited to join the school Poetry Society—a most anomalous organization for Charterhouse. It consisted of seven members. The meetings, for the reading and discussion of poetry, were held once a month. The other members were four sixth-form boys, and two boys a year and a half older than me.

Thus began a friendship between me and Raymond Rodakowski, one of the two younger members. Coming home one evening from a meeting of the society, I told Raymond about life in the house. A week or two before, my study had been raided. He suggested: 'You're not allowed to play football; why don't you box? It's supposed to improve the heart.' I laughed and promised that I would. Then Raymond asked: 'I expect they rag you about your initials?'

'Yes, they call me a dirty German.' 'I had trouble, too,' he told me, 'before I took up boxing.' Raymond's mother was Scottish; his father an Austrian Pole, a founder of the Brooklands Racing Track.

Very few boys boxed, and the boxing-room, over the school tuckshop, made a convenient place to meet Raymond. I began boxing seriously and savagely. Raymond said: 'These cricketers and footballers are all afraid of boxers, almost superstitious. They won't box themselves for fear of losing their good looks—the annual inter-house competitions are such bloody affairs. But do you remember the Mansfield, Waller and Taylor show? That's a useful tradition to keep up.'

Of course, I remembered. Two terms previously, there had been a famous meeting of the school Debating Society, the committee of which consisted of sixth-form boys. Though the debates were pretty dull, what passed for intellectual life at Charterhouse was represented by the Debating Society, and by *The Carthusian*, always edited by two members of this committee—both institutions being free from the control of masters. One Saturday debate-night the usual decorous conventions were broken by a riotous entry of 'bloods'— members of the cricket and football elevens. The bloods were the ruling caste at Charterhouse; the eleventh man in the Football Eleven, though he might be a member of the under-fourth form, enjoyed far more prestige than the most brilliant scholar in the sixth. Even 'Head of the School' was an empty title. But the sixth-form intellectuals and the bloods never fought. The bloods had nothing to gain by a clash; the intellectuals were happy to be left alone. So this invasion of the bloods, just returned from winning an 'away' match against the *Casuals*, and full of beer, caused the Debating Society a good deal of embarrassment. The bloods disturbed the meeting by cheers and cat-calls, and slammed the library magazine-folders on the table. Mansfield, as president of the society, called them to order, and when they continued the disturbance, closed the debate.

The bloods thought the incident finished, but they thought wrong. A letter appeared in *The Carthusian* a few days later, protesting against the bad behaviour in the Debating Society of 'certain First Eleven babies'. The three sets of initials signed were those of Mansfield, Waller and Taylor. The school, astonished by this suicidally daring act, waited for them to be swallowed up. The Captain of Football swore that he'd chuck the three signatories into the fountain in Founder's Court. But somehow he did not. The fact was that this happened early in the autumn term, and only two other First Eleven colours had been left over from the preceding year; new colours were given gradually as the football season advanced. The other rowdies had been merely embryo bloods. So the matter had to be settled between these three sixth-form intellectuals and the three colours of the First Eleven. But the First Eleven were uncomfortably aware that Mansfield was the heavy-weight boxing champion of the school, Waller the runner-up for the middle-weights, and that Taylor was also a tough fellow to be reckoned with. While they were wondering what on earth to do, Mansfield decided to take the war into his enemies' country.

The social code of Charterhouse rested on a strict caste system; the caste marks being slight distinctions in dress. A new boy had no privileges at all; a boy in his second term might wear a knitted tie instead of a plain one; a boy in his second year might wear coloured socks; the third year gave most of the main privileges—turned-down collars, coloured handkerchiefs, a coat with a long roll, and so on; fourth year, a few more, such as the right to get up raffles; but peculiar distinctions were reserved for the bloods. These included light-grey flannel trousers, butterfly collars, jackets slit up the back, and the right of walking arm-in-arm.

So the next Sunday Mansfield, Waller and Taylor did the

bravest deed ever done at Charterhouse. Chapel began at eleven in the morning, but the school had to be in its seats by five minutes to eleven and sit waiting there. At two minutes to eleven the bloods used to stalk up; at one and a half minutes to, came the masters; at one minute to, came the choir in their surplices; then the headmaster arrived, and the service began. If any boy, accidentally late, sneaked in between five minutes to, and two minutes to, the hour, six hundred pairs of eyes followed him; he heard whispering and giggling at his apparent foolhardiness in pretending to be a blood. On this Sunday, then, when the bloods had entered with their usual swaggering assurance, an extraordinary thing happened.

The three sixth-formers slowly walked up the aisle, magnificent in light-grey flannel trousers, slit jackets, butterfly collars, and each wore a pink carnation in his lapel. Astonished and horrified by this spectacle, everyone turned to gaze at the Captain of the First Eleven; he had gone quite white. But by this time the masters had entered, followed by the choir, and the opening hymn, though raggedly sung, ended the tension. When chapel emptied, it always emptied according to 'school order', that is, according to position in work: the sixth form therefore went out first. The bloods not being at all high in school order, Mansfield, Waller and Taylor had the start of them. After chapel on Sunday, the custom in the autumn term was for boys to meet and gossip in the library; so to the library Mansfield, Waller and Taylor went. On the way, they buttonholed a talkative master, drew him in with them and kept him talking until dinner-time. If the bloods had dared to do anything violent they would have had to do it at once, but to make a scene in the presence of a master was impossible. Mansfield, Waller and Taylor went down to their houses for dinner, still talking to the master. After that, they always went about together in public, and the school, particularly the lower school, which had long chafed under the dress regulations, made heroes of them and began scoffing at the bloods as weak-kneed.

Finally, the Captain of the Eleven complained to the headmaster about this breach of school conventions, asking for permission to enforce the bloods' rights by disciplinary measures. Rendall, the headmaster, was a scholar and disliked the games tradition. He refused his request, insisting that the sixth form deserved as distinctive privileges as the First Eleven, and were, in his opinion, entitled to hold what they had assumed. The prestige of the bloods declined greatly.

On Raymond's encouragement, I pulled myself together and when the next school year started found things very much easier. My chief persecutor, the Irishman, had gone away with a nervous breakdown. He wrote me a hysterical demand for forgiveness—saying at the same time that, if I refused it, he still had a friend in the house to give me a bad time. I did not answer the letter.

5

IN my fifth year at Charterhouse I reached the sixth form, and became a house-monitor. There were six of us. One of them, Jack Young, the house games-captain, a friendly, easy-going fellow, said one day: 'Look here, Graves, I have to send in a list of competitors for the inter-house boxing competitions; shall I put your name down?' By that time, boxing had rather lost its interest; I had been busy with football, and played for the house-team now. 'I'm not boxing these days,' I told Young. 'Well,' he said, 'young Alan is entering for the welter-weights. He's got a fair chance. Why don't you enter for the welter-weights too? You might be able to damage one or two of the stronger men, and make things easier for him.' I did not altogether like the idea of making things easier for Alan, but obviously I had to enter the competition. Realizing that my wind, though all right for football, would not be equal to boxing round after round, I decided that my fights must be short. The house-butler smuggled a bottle of cherry· whisky in for me—I would shorten the fights on that.

I had never drunk anything alcoholic before in my life. At seven years old my mother persuaded me to sign a pledge card, which bound me to abstain by the grace of God from all spirituous liquors so long as I retained it. But my mother took the card away and put it safely in the box-room with other family souvenirs, and since box-room treasures never left the box-room, I regarded myself as permanently parted from my pledge. This cherry-whisky delighted me.

The competitions began at about one o'clock on a Saturday afternoon, and went on until seven. I was drawn for the very first fight and my opponent, by ill-luck, was Alan—from my own house. Alan wanted me to scratch. I told him it would look bad to do so. We consulted Jack Young, who said: 'No, the most sporting thing will be to box it out, and let the decision be given on points; but don't either of you hurt each other!' So we boxed. Alan started showing off to his friends, who were sitting in the front row. I muttered: 'Stop that, we're boxing, not fighting!' but a few seconds later he hit me again, unnecessarily hard. I got angry and knocked him out with a right swing on the side of his neck. This was the first time I had ever knocked anyone out, and the feeling combined well with my cherry-whisky exaltation. I muzzily realized that the swing did not form part of the ordinary school-boxing curriculum. Straight lefts; lefts to body, rights to head; left and right hooks; all these were known, but the swing had somehow been neglected, probably because it was not so 'pretty'.

I went to the changing-room for my coat, and stout Sergeant Harris, the boxing instructor, said: 'Look here, Mr Graves, why don't you put down your name for the middle-weight competition too?' I cheerfully agreed. Then I went back to the house, where I took a cold bath and more cherry-whisky. My next fight, for the first round of the middle-weights, would take place half an hour later. This time my opponent, who was a stone heavier than myself but had little science, bustled me about for the first round, and I could see that he would tire me out unless I did something pretty soon. In the second round I knocked him down with my right swing, but he got up. Feeling a bit winded, I hastened to knock him down again. I must have knocked him down four or five times that round, but he refused to take the count. Finally I thought, as he lurched towards me once more: 'If you don't go down, and stay down, this time, I won't be able to hit you again at all.' I just pushed at his jaw as it offered itself to me, but that was enough. He went down, and he stayed down. This second knock-out made quite a stir. Knock-outs were rare in these boxing competitions. As I returned to the house for another cold bath and some more cherry-whisky, I noticed the fellows looking at me curiously, almost with admiration.

The later stages of the competition are vague in my memory. I now had to worry only about Raymond—nearly a stone heavier than myself, and expected to win the middle-weights; but he had also gone in for two weights, the middle and the heavy, and just been through a tough fight with the eventual winner of the heavy-weights, that left him in no proper state to continue. So he scratched his fight with me. I believe that Raymond would have fought all the same, had it been against anyone else; but he wanted me to win, and knew that his scratching would give me a rest between bouts. Then a semi-finalist scratched against me in the welter-weights, so only three more fights remained, and I let none of them go beyond the first round. The swing won me both weights, for which I received two silver cups. But I had also dislocated both my thumbs by not getting my elbow high enough over. When I tried to sell the cups some years later, to keep food in my mouth, they turned out to be only silver-plated.

In my last year at Charterhouse I did everything possible to show how little respect I had for school tradition. In the winter of 1913 I won a classical exhibition at St John's College, Oxford, which allowed me to go slow on school-work. One of my last recollections at Charterhouse is a school debate on the motion 'that this house is in favour of compulsory military service'. The Empire Service League, with Earl Roberts of Kandahar, V.C., as its President, sent down a propagandist in support. Only six votes out of one hundred and nineteen were noes. I was the principal opposition speaker, having recently resigned from the Officers' Training Corps in revolt against the theory of implicit obedience to orders. And during a fortnight spent the previous summer at the O.T.C. camp near Tidworth on Salisbury Plain, I had been frightened by a special display of the latest military fortifications: barbed-wire entanglements, machine-guns, and field artillery in action. General, now Field-Marshal Sir William Robertson, who had a son at the school, visited the camp and impressed upon us that war with Germany must inevitably break out within two or three years, and that we must be prepared to take our part in it as leaders of the new forces which would assuredly be called into being. Of the six noes, Nevill Barbour and I are, I believe, the only ones who survived the war.

My last memory is the headmaster's parting shot: 'Well, goodbye, Graves, and remember that your best friend is the waste-paper basket.' This has proved good advice, though not perhaps in the sense he intended: few writers seem to send their work through as many drafts as I do.

I used to speculate on which of my contemporaries would distinguish themselves after they left school. The war upset these calculations. Many dull boys had brief brilliant military careers, particularly as air-fighters, becoming squadron and flight commanders. 'Fuzzy' McNair, the Head of the school, won the V.C. as a Rifleman. Young Sturgess, who had been my study fag, distinguished himself more unfortunately by flying the first heavy bombing machine of a new pattern across the Channel on his first trip to France: he made a perfect landing (having mistaken his course) at an aerodrome behind the German lines. A boy whom I had admired during my first year at Charterhouse was the Honourable Desmond O'Brien: the only Carthusian of that time who cheerfully disregarded all school rules. Having cut skeleton-keys for the library, chapel, and science laboratories, he used to break out of his house at night and carefully disarrange things there. O'Brien had the key to the headmaster's study too and, entering one night with an electric torch, carried off a memorandum which he showed me: 'Must expel O'Brien.' He had a wireless receiving station in one of the out-of-bounds copses on the school grounds; and discovered a ventilator shaft down which he could hoot like an owl into the library without detection. Once we were threatened with the loss of a half-holiday because some member of the school had catapulted a cow, which died of shock, and nobody would own up. O'Brien was away at the time, on special leave for a sister's wedding. A friend wrote to tell him about the half-holiday. He sent the headmaster a telegram: 'Killed cow sorry coming O'Brien.' At last Rendall did expel him for having absented himself from every lesson and chapel for three whole days. O'Brien was killed, early in the war, while bombing Bruges.

At least one in three of my generation at school died; because they all took commissions as soon as they could, most of them in the infantry and Royal Flying Corps. The average life expectancy of an infantry subaltern on the Western Front was, at some stages of the war, only about three months; by which time he had been either wounded or killed. The proportions worked out at about four wounded to every one killed. Of these four, one got wounded seriously, and the remaining three more or less slightly. The three lightly wounded returned to the front after a few weeks or months of absence, and again faced the same odds. Flying casualties were even higher. Since the war lasted for four and a half years, it is easy to see why most of the survivors, if not permanently disabled, got wounded several times.

6

I HAD just finished with Charterhouse when England declared war on Germany A day or two later I decided to enlist. In the first place, though the papers predicted only a very short war—over by Christmas at the outside—I hoped that it might last long enough to delay my going to Oxford in October, which I dreaded. Nor did I work out the possibilities of getting actively engaged in the fighting, expecting garrison service at home while the regular forces were away. In the second place, I was outraged to read of the Germans' cynical violation of Belgian neutrality. Though I discounted perhaps twenty per cent of the atrocity details as wartime exaggeration, that was not, of course, sufficient. Recently I saw the following contemporary newspaper cuttings put in chronological sequence:

> When the fall of Antwerp became known, the church bells were rung (i.e. at Cologne and elsewhere in Germany). —*Kölnische Zeitung.*

> According to the *Kölnische Zeitung*, the clergy of Antwerp were compelled to ring the church bells when the fortress was taken.—*Le Matin.*

> According to what *The Times* has heard from Cologne, via

Paris, the unfortunate Belgian priests who refused to ring the church bells when Antwerp was taken, have been sentenced to hard labour.—*Corriere della Sera*.

According to information which has reached the *Corriere della Sera* from Cologne, *via* London, it is confirmed that the barbaric conquerors of Antwerp punished the unfortunate Belgian priests for their heroic refusal to ring the church bells by hanging them as living clappers to the bells with their heads down.—*Le Matin*.

In the trenches, a few months later, I happened to belong to a company mess in which four of us young officers out of five had, by a coincidence, either German mothers or naturalized German fathers. One of them said: 'I'm glad I joined when I did. If I'd put it off for a month or two, they'd have accused me of being a German spy. As it is, I have an uncle interned in Alexandra Palace, and my father's only been allowed to retain the membership of his golf club because he has two sons in the trenches.' I told him: 'Well, I have three or four uncles sitting somewhere opposite, and a number of cousins, too. One of those uncles is a general. But that's all right. I don't brag about them. I only advertise my uncle Dick Poore, the British admiral commanding at the Nore.'

Among these enemy relatives was my cousin Conrad, only son of the German Consul at Zürich. In January 1914, I had gone ski-ing with him between the trees in the woods above the city. And once we tobogganed together down the Dolderstrasse in Zürich itself, where the lamp-posts were sandbagged and family toboggans, skidding broadside on at the turns, were often crashed into by single-seater skeletons; arms and legs got broken by the score, and the crowds thought it a great joke. Conrad served with a crack Bavarian regiment throughout the war, and won the 'Pour le Mérite', an order even more rarely awarded than the British Victoria

Cross. Soon after the war ended, a party of Bolsheviks killed him in a Baltic village, where he had been sent to make requisitions. Conrad was a gentle, proud creature, chiefly interested in natural history, who used to spend hours in the woods studying the habits of wild animals; he had strong feelings against shooting them.

Perhaps my family's most outstanding military feat was a German uncle's; he had been dug out at the age of forty-five as a lieutenant in the Bavarian artillery. My brother John met him a year or two ago, and happened to mention a coming visit to Rheims. My uncle nudged him: 'Have a look at the cathedral. One day, during the war, my divisional general called for me. "Gunner-lieutenant von Ranke, I understand that you are a Lutheran, not a Roman Catholic?" I admitted this was so. Then he said: "I have a very disagreeable service for you to perform, Lieutenant. Those misbegotten French are using the cathedral for an observation post. They think they can get away with it because it's Rheims Cathedral, but they have our trenches taped from there. I call upon you to dislodge them." I fired only two rounds, and down came the pinnacle and the Frenchmen with it. A very neat bit of shooting. I felt proud to have limited the damage like that. Really, you must take a look at it.'

The Harlech golf club secretary suggested my taking a commission instead of enlisting. He rang up the nearest regimental depôt—the Royal Welch Fusiliers at Wrexham—and told the adjutant that I had served in the Officers Training Corps at Charterhouse. The adjutant said: 'Send him right along.' On August 11th I began my training, and immediately became a hero. My mother announced: 'Our race has gone mad!' and regarded my going as a religious act; my father felt proud that I had 'done the right thing'.

Most of the other applicants for commissions at Wrexham were boys who had recently failed to pass into the Royal Military College at Sandhurst, and were now trying to get into the regular army at the old militia back-door—re-named the Special Reserve. Only one or two fellows had come, like myself, for the sake of the war, and not for the sake of a career. There were about a dozen of us recruit officers on the Square, learning to drill and be drilled. My O.T.C. experience helped me here, but I knew nothing of Army tradition and made all the worst mistakes—saluting the bandmaster, failing to recognize the colonel when in mufti, walking in the street without a belt, talking shop in the mess. Though I soon learned to conform, my greatest difficulty was addressing the men of my platoon with the proper air of authority. Many of them were re-enlisted old soldiers, and I disliked bluffing that I knew more than they did. We had two or three very old soldiers employed on the depôt staff, wearing ribbons of Burma, 1885, and even earlier campaigns, and usually also the ribbon of the 'Rooti', or good service, medal awarded for 'eighteen years of undetected crime'. Of one old fellow, called Jackie Barrett, a Kipling character, I heard it said: 'There goes Jackie Barrett. He and his chum deserted the regiment at Quetta, and crossed the North-West Frontier on foot. Three months later, Jackie gave himself up as a deserter to the British Consul in Jerusalem. He buried his chum on the way.'

After only three weeks on the Square, I went off on detachment duty, to a newly-formed internment camp for enemy aliens at Lancaster. The camp was a disused wagon-works near the river, a dirty, draughty place, littered with old scrap metal and guarded by high barbed-wire fences. About three thousand prisoners had already arrived there, and more and more crowded in every day: seamen arrested on German vessels in Liverpool harbour, waiters from large hotels in the north, an odd German band or two, harmless German commercial travellers and shopkeepers. The prisoners resented being interned, particularly family men who had lived at peace in England for many years. The one comfort that we could offer them was: 'You are safer inside than out.' For anti-German feeling had begun to run high; shops with German names were continually raided; and even German women made to feel that they were personally responsible for the alleged Belgian atrocities. Besides, we pointed out, in Germany they would be forced to join the Army. At this time, we could make a boast of our voluntary system, and never foresaw the time when these internees would be bitterly envied by forcibly-enlisted Englishmen for being kept safe until the war ended.

In the summer of 1915, *The Times* reprinted a German newspaper account by Herr Wolff, an exchanged prisoner, of his experiences at Lancaster in 1914. *The Times* amused itself with Wolff's allegations that he and forty other waiters from the Midland Hotel, Manchester, had been arrested and taken, handcuffed and fettered, in special railway carriages to Lancaster, escorted by fifty Manchester policemen armed with carbines. But it was true, because I myself took them over from the Chief Inspector, a fine figure in a frogged tunic, who gave me a splendid salute. He had done his job well and seemed proud of it, the only mishap being the accidental breaking of two carriage windows by the slung carbines. Wolff reported that even children were interned in the camp; and this also was true. A dozen or so little boys from the German bands had been interned because it seemed more humane to keep them with their friends than to send them to a workhouse.

I commanded a detachment of fifty Special Reservists, most of them with only six weeks' service; a rough lot of Welshmen from the border counties. They had joined the Army just before war started, as a cheap way of getting a training-camp holiday; being forced to continue beyond the usual fortnight exasperated them. They were constantly deserting and having to be fetched back by the police, and seemed more scared of the prisoners than the prisoners were of them. I hated doing my round of sentries on a dark night at 2 or 3 a.m.

33

Very often the lantern used to blow out and, fumbling to light it again in the dark, I would hear the frightened voice of a sentry roar: 'Halt! Who goes there?' I knew that he would be standing with his rifle aimed and five live rounds in his magazine; but always gave him the pass-word just in time. Sentries often fired at shadows. The prisoners, particularly the sailors, fought a good deal among themselves. I saw a prisoner spit out teeth and blood one morning, and asked him what was wrong. 'Oh, sir, one no-good friend give me one clap on the chops.' Frequent deputations came to complain of the dullness of the food—the same ration food served to the troops. But after a while the prisoners settled down to sullen docility, starting hobbies, glee parties, games, and plans for escape. I had far more trouble with my Welshmen, who were always escaping from their quarters, though I guarded all possible exits. Finally I discovered that they had been crawling through a sewer.

An inconvenient accident happened to me at Lancaster. The telephone was installed at an office where I slept on a sloping desk. One night, Pack Saddle (the code name for the Chief Supply Officer, Western Command) rang up from Chester after midnight, with orders for the commandant. They concerned the rationing of another batch of four hundred prisoners, who were being sent to him from Chester and North Wales. In the middle of a conversation made difficult by a thunderstorm, my sleepiness, and Pack Saddle's irritability, the line got struck by lightning somewhere. An electric shock spun me round, and I could not use a telephone again without sweating and stammering until some twelve years later.

Guarding prisoners seemed an unheroic part to be playing in the war which, by October, had reached a critical stage; I wanted to be abroad fighting. My training had been interrupted, and I knew that even when recalled from detachment duty, I should have to wait a month or two at least before getting sent out. When I returned to the depôt, 'Tibs' Crawshay, the adjutant, a keen regular soldier, found two things wrong with me. First of all—I had not only gone to an inefficient tailor, but also had a soldier-servant who neglected to polish my buttons and shine my belt and boots as he should have done. Never having owned a valet before, I did not know what to expect of him. Crawshay finally summoned me to the Orderly Room. He would not send me to France, he said, until I had entirely overhauled my wardrobe and looked more like a soldier—my company commander's report on me was 'unsoldierlike and a nuisance'. But my pay only just covered the mess bills, and I could hardly ask my parents to buy me another outfit so soon after assuring them that I had everything necessary. Crawshay next decided that I must be a poor sportsman—probably because on the day of the Grand National, in which a horse of his was running, all the young officers applied for leave to see the race, except myself. I volunteered to take the job of Orderly Officer for the Day for someone who wanted to go.

One by one my contemporaries were sent out to France to take the place of casualties in the First and Second Battalions, while I remained despondently at the depôt. But again boxing helped me. Johnny Basham, a sergeant in the regiment, was training at the time for his fight—which he won—with Boswell for the Lonsdale Belt, welter-weight. I visited the training camp one evening, where Basham was offering to fight three rounds with any member of the regiment—the more the merrier. A young officer pulled on the gloves, and Basham got roars of laughter from the crowd as soon as he had taken his opponent's measure, by dodging around and playing the fool with him. I asked Basham's manager if I could have a go. He lent me some shorts, and I stepped into the ring. Pretending to know nothing of boxing, I led off with my right and moved clumsily. Basham saw a chance of getting another laugh; he dropped his guard and danced about with a you-can't-hit-me challenge. I caught him off his balance, and knocked him across the ring. He recovered and went for me, but I managed to keep on my feet. When I laughed at him, he laughed too. We had three very brisk rounds, and he very decently made me seem a much better boxer than I was, by accommodating his pace to mine. As soon as Crawshay heard the story, he rang me up at my billet and told me that he had learned with pleasure of my performance; that for an officer to box like that was a great encouragement for the men; that he was mistaken about my sportsmanship; and that, to show his appreciation, he would put me down for a draft to France in a week's time.

One or two random memories remain of this training period at Wrexham. The landlord of my billet, a Welsh solicitor, greatly overcharged us through pretending amicability. He wore a wig—or, to be more exact, three wigs, with hair of progressive lengths. After wearing the medium-sized hair for a few days, he would put on the long-haired wig, and say that, dear him! he really ought to get a hair-cut. Then he would leave the house and, in a public lavatory perhaps, or a wayside copse, change into the short-haired wig, which he wore until he thought it time to change to the medium once more. The deception came to light when one of the officers billeted with me got drunk and raided his bedroom.

Recruit officers spent a good deal of their time at Company and Battalion Orderly Room, learning how to deal with crime. 'Crime' meant any breach of King's Regulations; and there was plenty of it. Battalion Orderly Room would last for four or five hours every day, at the rate of one crime dealt with every three or four minutes—this being apart from the scores of less serious offences tried by company commanders. The usual Battalion Orderly Room crimes were desertion, refusing to obey an order, using obscene language to a non-commissioned officer, drunk and disorderly, robbing a comrade, and so forth. On pay-nights, hardly a man stayed sober;

but no attention was paid if silence reigned as soon as the company officer came on his rounds at Lights Out. Two years later, serious crime had diminished to a twentieth of that amount, though the battalion was treble its original strength, and though many of the cases that the company officer had dealt with summarily, now came before the colonel; and drunkenness practically vanished.

Orderly Room always embarrassed and dispirited me. I never got used to it, even after sentencing thousands of men myself. The greatest number of simultaneous charges that I ever heard brought against a soldier occurred in the case of Boy Jones, at Liverpool in 1917. They accused him, first, of using obscene language to the bandmaster. (The bandmaster, who was squeamish, reported it as: 'Sir, he called me a double effing c——.') Next, breaking out of the detention awarded for this crime. Then, 'absenting himself from the regiment until apprehended in the Hindenburg Line, France'. Fourth, resisting an escort. Fifth, being found in possession of regimental property belonging to the Cheshire Regiment. Boy Jones, who was only fourteen, and looked thirteen, had wriggled through the bars of his detention-cell and, after getting a few things together in his hut, gone to Liverpool Exchange Station to wait for a victim—who proved to be a private in a Cheshire Bantam Battalion, just returning to France from leave. Bantam Battalions consisted of volunteers hitherto too short to qualify for the Army. Boy Jones treated the bantam to a lot of drink and robbed him of his rifle, equipment, badges and papers. He then went off in his place. Arrived in France, he proceeded to the Bantam Battalion; but this did not suit him. He wanted to be with his own regiment; so he deserted the Bantams, who were billeted somewhere north of Arras, and walked south along the trenches looking for his regiment, having now resumed his proper badges. A couple of days' walk brought him to the Second Battalion Headquarters where he reported, but was immediately sent home, after a tough struggle with his escort at the railhead. The punishment awarded for all these heinous offences—'ten days confined to camp', and a spanking by the bandmaster— seemed to us very nicely calculated.

At Wrexham, we second-lieutenants learned regimental history, drill, musketry, Boer War field-tactics, military law and organization, how to recognize bugle calls, how to work a machine-gun, and how to conduct ourselves on formal occasions. We dug no trenches, handled no bombs, and thought of the company, not of the platoon, still less of the section, as the smallest independent tactical unit. Only two wounded officers were back from the front at the time; both had left the Second Battalion on the retreat from Mons. Neither would talk much of his experiences.

7

I USED to congratulate myself on having quite blindly chosen
the Royal Welch Fusiliers, of all regiments in the Army.
The Royal Welch had twenty-nine battle-honours, a number
equalled only by a couple of other two-battalion regiments.
The First Battalion of the Royal Welch Fusiliers could boast
twenty-six battle-honours of its own, the remaining three
having fallen to the Second Battalion in its short and interrupted existence. They were all good bloody battle-honours,
none of them like that battle into which, it was said, the Argyll
and Sutherland Highlanders had gone with nine hundred men
and from which they emerged with nine hundred and one—
no casualties, and a band-boy come of age and promoted a
private.

I caught the sense of regimental tradition a day or two after
my arrival at the depôt. In a cupboard at the mess, I came
across a big leather-bound ledger and pulled it out to read.
It proved to be the Daily Order Book of the First Battalion
in the trenches before Sevastopol, and I opened it at the page
giving orders for an attack on the Redan Redoubt. Such and
such a company was desired to supply volunteers for the
storming party under Lieutenant So-and-so. Next followed
details of their arms and equipment, the number of ladders
they must carry, and the support to be afforded by other

companies. Then details of rations and supply of ammunition, with an earnest 'Godspeed!' from the commanding officer. (A sketch of the commanding officer hung on the wall above my head, lying sick in his tent at Scutari, wearing a 'Balaclava helmet', or cap-comforter, against the intense cold.) The attack failed, and among subsequent entries were orders for the burial of the dead, appreciation from headquarters of the gallantry vainly displayed, and a notice that the effects of Lieutenant So-and-so, who had led the storming party, would be sold at public auction in the trenches next day. Another Daily Order contained the citation of a certain Sergeant Luke O'Connor's gallantry, for which he received one of the first Victoria Crosses when the award was instituted in 1856. He still lived—Lieutenant-General Sir Luke O'Connor, now Colonel of the Regiment.

The most immediate piece of regimental history that I met as a recruit-officer was the flash: a fan-like bunch of five black ribbons, each two inches wide, seven and a half inches long, and ending in a dove-tail. The angle at which the fan must be spread has been exactly regulated by regimental convention. The flash is stitched to the back of the tunic collar, and only the Royal Welch are privileged to wear it. The story goes that the Royal Welch were abroad on foreign service for several years in the 1830s, and by some mischance never received the Army order abolishing the queue. When the regiment returned and paraded at Plymouth, the inspecting general reprimanded the commanding officer because his men were still wearing their hair in the old fashion. The commanding officer, angered by the slight, immediately rode up to London and won from King William IV, through the intercession of some Court official, a regimental privilege of continuing to wear the bunch of ribbons with which the end of the queue was tied—the flash. The King made it a distinctive badge to be worn by all ranks in recognition of exemplary service during the Napoleonic Wars.

40

The Army Council, which is usually composed of cavalry, engineer, artillery and Guards generals, with the Line hardly represented, had never encouraged regimental peculiarities, and could not easily forget the irregularity of our direct appeal to the Sovereign. The Army Council did not, at any rate, sanction the flash on the new khaki service-dress. Yet our officers and warrant-officers continued to wear it. In a pre-war correspondence between the regiment and the Army Council, Sir Luke O'Connor maintained that the flash, being a distinctive mark honourably won, should be worn with service-dress, and not merely with peacetime scarlet. The Army Council objected that it would be a distinctive mark for enemy snipers, and particularly dangerous when worn by officers. Sir Luke retorted by inquiring on what occasion, since the retreat from Corunna, when the regiment was the last to leave Spain, with the key of the town postern in the pocket of one of its officers, had any of His Majesty's enemies seen the back of a Royal Welch Fusilier officer? The Army Council stood firm; and the matter remained in abeyance throughout the war. Once, in 1917, when an officer of my company went to be decorated with the Military Cross at Buckingham Palace, King George, as Colonel-in-Chief of the regiment, showed a personal interest in the flash. He asked: 'You are serving in one of the line battalions?' 'The Second Battalion, sir.' So the King gave him the order 'About turn!' for a look at the flash, and then 'About turn!' again. 'Good,' he said, 'you're still wearing it, I see,' and then, in a stage whisper: 'Don't ever let anyone take it from you!'

After the war, when scarlet was abandoned on the grounds of expense, the Army Council saw that it could now reasonably sanction the flash on service-dress for all ranks. As an additional favour it consented to recognize another defiant regimental peculiarity: the spelling of the word 'Welch' with a *c*. This permission was published in a special Army Council Instruction of 1919. The spelling with a *c* was as important to

us as the miniature cap-badge worn at the back of the cap was
to the Gloucesters (a commemoration of the time when they
fought back to back in Egypt). I have seen a young officer
sent off Battalion Parade because his buttons read 'Welsh'
instead of 'Welch'. 'Welch' referred us somehow to the
archaic North Wales of Henry Tudor and Owen Glendower
and Lord Herbert of Cherbury, the founder of the regiment;
it dissociated us from the modern North Wales of chapels,
Liberalism, the dairy and drapery business, slate mines, and
the tourist trade.

The regiment insisted strictly on the standard measurement
of the flash. When New Army battalions were formed, and
rumours came to Wrexham that in the Eighteenth Battalion
officers were wearing flashes nearly down to their waists,
great consternation ensued. Our adjutant sent off the youngest
subaltern on a special mission to the Eighteenth Battalion,
the colonel of which had been borrowed from some Yorkshire
regiment. The subaltern had orders to present himself at the
Orderly Room with a large pair of shears.

On arrival at the depôt, we Special Reserve officers were
reminded of our great good fortune: if the war lasted, we
should have the privilege of serving with one or the other of
the line battalions. In peacetime, a candidate for a commission
had not only to distinguish himself in the passing-out examination at the Royal Military College, Sandhurst, and be strongly
recommended by two officers of the regiment, but to possess
a guaranteed independent income that would enable him to
play polo and hunt and keep up the social reputation of the
regiment. These requirements were waived in our case; but
we were to understand that we did not belong to the 'Regiment' in the special sense. Permission to serve with it in time
of war should satisfy our highest military aspirations. We
were not temporary officers, like those of the New Army, but
held permanent commissions in the Special Reserve Battalion.
The Royal Welch, we were reminded, considered themselves

second to none, even to the Guards. Representations had been made to them, after the South African War, inquiring whether they would like to become the Welsh Guards, and the offer had been indignantly declined; such a change would have made the regiment junior, in the brigade, even to the recently formed Irish Guards.

We were warned that while serving with a line battalion, none of us must expect to be recommended for orders or decorations. An ordinary campaigning medal, inscribed with a record of battalion service, should suffice as reward. Decorations were not considered by the Royal Welch as personal awards, but as representative awards for the whole regiment. They would therefore be kept for the professional soldiers, who would find them useful as aids to extra-regimental promotion. This was what, in fact, happened. There must have been something like two or three hundred Special Reserve officers serving overseas with the regiment before the war ended. But except for a few of us, who were not directly recommended by the battalion commander, but distinguished themselves while attached to brigade or divisional staffs, or who got sent to New Army battalions or other regiments, we continued undecorated. I can recall only three exceptions. The normal proportion of awards, considering the casualties we suffered, which was about sixty or seventy killed, should have been at least ten times that amount. Let me hasten to say that I myself never performed any feat for which I might conceivably have been decorated throughout my service in France.

The regimental spirit persistently survived all catastrophes. Our First Battalion, for instance, was practically annihilated within two months of joining the British Expeditionary Force. Young Orme, who joined straight from Sandhurst, at the crisis of the first battle of Ypres, found himself commanding a battalion reduced to only about forty rifles. With these, and another small force, the remnants of the Second Battalion of

D

the Queen's Regiment, reduced to thirty men and two officers, he helped to recapture three lines of lost trenches and was himself killed. The reconstituted battalion saw heavy fighting at Bois Grenier in December, but got smashed up at the Aubers Ridge and Festubert in the following May; and again at Loos in September, when only one combatant officer survived the attack—a machine-gun officer on loan from the South Staffordshire Regiment. The same sort of thing happened time after time in fighting at Fricourt, the Quadrangle, High Wood, Delville Wood, and Ginchy on the Somme in 1916; and again at Puisieux and Bullecourt in the spring fighting of 1917; and again, and again, until the Armistice. In the course of the war, at least fifteen or twenty thousand men must have passed through each of the two line battalions, whose fighting strength never stood at more than eight hundred. After each catastrophe the ranks were filled up with new drafts from home, with the lightly wounded from the disaster of three or four months before, and with the more seriously wounded of earlier ones.

In the First and Second Battalions, throughout the war, not merely the officers and N.C.O.s knew their regimental history. The men had learned far more about Minden, Albuhera and Waterloo, and the Battle of the Pyramids, than they had about the fighting on the other fronts, or the official causes of the war.

8

O<small>N</small> arrival in France, we six Royal Welch Fusilier officers went to the Harfleur base-camp near Le Havre. Later it became an educational centre for trench routine, use of bombs, trench-mortars, rifle-grenades, gas-helmets, and similar technicalities. But now we did a route-march or two through the French countryside and that was all, apart from fatigues at the Le Havre docks, helping the Army Service Corps unload stores from ships. I was glad when we got orders to go 'up the line', though disgusted to find ourselves posted not to the Royal Welch Fusiliers, but to the Welsh Regiment.

I had heard little about the Welsh Regiment, except that it was tough and rough. In Cardiff the Welsh Regiment advertised: 'Enlist at the depôt and get to France quick.' The recruits were mostly men either over-age or under-age or with some slight physical disability which prevented them from enlisting in regiments more particular than the Welsh.

I still have the roll of my first platoon of forty men. The figures given for their ages are misleading. On enlistment, all over-age men had put themselves in the late thirties, and all under-age men had called themselves eighteen. But once in France, the over-age men did not mind adding on a few genuine years. No less than fourteen in the roll gave their age as forty or over, and these were not all. Fred Prosser, a painter in civil life, who admitted to forty-eight, was really fifty-six. David Davies, collier, who admitted to forty-two, and Thomas Clark, another collier who admitted to forty-five, were only one or two years junior to Prosser. James Burford, collier and fitter, was the oldest soldier of all. When I first spoke to him in the trenches, he said: 'Excuse me, sir, will you explain what this here arrangement is on the side of my rifle?' 'That's the safety-catch. Didn't you do a musketry-course at the depôt?' 'No, sir, I was a re-enlisted man, and I spent only a fortnight there. The old Lee-Metford didn't have no safety-catch.' I asked him when he had last fired a rifle. 'In Egypt, in 1882,' he said. 'Weren't you in the South African War?' 'I tried to re-enlist, but they told me I was too old, sir. I had been an old soldier in Egypt. My real age is sixty-three.' He spent all his summers as a tramp, and in the bad months of the year worked as a collier, choosing a new pit every season. I heard him and David Davies one night discussing the different seams of coal in Wales, and tracing them from county to county and pit to pit with technical comments.

The other half of the platoon contained the under-age section. I had five of these boys: William Bumford, collier, for instance, who gave his age as eighteen, was really only fifteen. He used to get into trouble for falling asleep on sentry duty, an offence punishable with death, but could not help it. I had seen him suddenly go to sleep, on his feet, while holding a sandbag open for another fellow to fill. So we got him a job as orderly to a chaplain for a while, and a few months later all men over fifty and all boys under eighteen got combed out. Bumford and Burford were both sent to the base; but neither escaped the war. Bumford grew old enough by 1917 to be sent back to the battalion, and was killed that summer; Burford died in a bombing accident at the base-camp. Or so I was told —the fate of hundreds of my comrades in France came to me merely as hearsay.

The troop-train consisted of forty-seven coaches, and took

twenty-four hours to arrive at Béthune, the railhead, via St Omer. We detrained at about 9 p.m., hungry, cold and dirty. Expecting a short journey, we had allowed our baggage to be locked in a van; and then played nap throughout the journey to keep our minds off the discomfort. I lost sixty francs, which was over two pounds at the existing rate of exchange. On the platform at Béthune, a little man in filthy khaki, wearing the Welsh cap-badge, came up with a friendly touch of the cap most unlike a salute. He had orders to guide us to the battalion, at present in the Cambrin trenches, about ten kilometres away. Collecting the draft of forty men we had with us, we followed him through the unlit suburbs of the town—all intensely excited by the noise and flashes of the guns in the distance. None of the draft had been out before, except the sergeant in charge. They began singing. Instead of the usual music-hall songs they sang Welsh hymns, each man taking a part. The Welsh always sang when pretending not to be scared; it kept them steady. And they never sang out of tune.

We marched towards the flashes, and could soon see the flare-lights curving across the distant trenches. The noise of the guns grew louder and louder. Presently we were among the batteries. From about two hundred yards behind us, on the left of the road, a salvo of four shells whizzed suddenly over our heads. This broke up *Aberystwyth* in the middle of a verse, and sent us off our balance for a few seconds; the column of fours tangled up. The shells went hissing away eastward; we saw the red flash and heard the hollow bang where they landed in German territory. The men picked up their step again and began chaffing. A lance-corporal dictated a letter home: 'Dear auntie, this leaves me in the pink. We are at present wading in blood up to our necks. Send me fags and a life-belt. This war is a booger. Love and kisses.'

The roadside cottages were now showing more and more signs of dilapidation. A German shell came over and then whoo—oo—ooooOO—bump——CRASH! landed twenty yards short of us. We threw ourselves flat on our faces. Presently we heard a curious singing noise in the air, and then flop! flop! little pieces of shell-casing came buzzing down all around. 'They calls them the musical instruments,' said the sergeant. 'Damn them,' said my friend Frank Jones-Bateman, cut across the hand by a jagged little piece, 'the devils have started on me early.' 'Aye, they'll have a lot of fun with you before they're done, sir,' grinned the sergeant. Another shell came over. Everyone threw himself down again, but it burst two hundred yards behind us. Only Sergeant Jones had remained on his feet. 'You're wasting your strength, lads,' he said to the draft. 'Listen by the noise they make where they're going to burst.'

At Cambrin village, about a mile from the front trenches, we were taken into a ruined chemist's shop with its coloured glass jars still in the window: the billet of the four Welsh company quartermaster-sergeants. Here they gave us respirators and field-dressings. This, the first respirator issued in France, was a gauze-pad filled with chemically-treated cotton waste, for tying across the mouth and nose. Reputedly it could not keep out the German gas, which had been used at Ypres against the Canadian Division; but we never put it to the test. A week or two later came the 'smoke-helmet', a greasy grey-felt bag with a talc window to look through, and no mouthpiece, certainly ineffective against gas. The talc was always cracking, and visible leaks showed at the stitches joining it to the helmet.

Those were early days of trench warfare, the days of the jam-tin bomb and the gas-pipe trench-mortar: still innocent of Lewis or Stokes guns, steel helmets, telescopic rifle-sights, gas-shells, pill-boxes, tanks, well-organized trench-raids, or any of the later refinements of trench warfare.

After a meal of bread, bacon, rum, and bitter stewed tea sickly with sugar, we went through the broken trees to the east of the village and up a long trench to battalion headquarters. The wet and slippery trench ran through dull red clay. I had a torch with me, and saw that hundreds of field mice and frogs had fallen into the trench but found no way out. The light dazzled them, and because I could not help treading on them, I put the torch back in my pocket. We had no mental picture of what the trenches would be like, and were almost as ignorant as a young soldier who joined us a week or two later. He called out excitedly to old Burford, who was cooking up a bit of stew in a dixie, apart from the others: 'Hi, mate, where's the battle? I want to do my bit.'

The guide gave us hoarse directions all the time. 'Hole right.' 'Wire high.' 'Wire low.' 'Deep place here, sir.' 'Wire low.' The field-telephone wires had been fastened by staples to the side of the trench, and when it rained the staples were constantly falling out and the wire falling down and tripping people up. If it sagged too much, one stretched it across the trench to the other side to correct the sag, but then it would catch one's head. The holes were sump-pits used for draining the trenches.

We now came under rifle-fire, which I found more trying than shell-fire. The gunner, I knew, fired not at people but at map-references—crossroads, likely artillery positions, houses that suggested billets for troops, and so on. Even when an observation officer in an aeroplane or captive balloon or on a church spire directed the guns, it seemed random, somehow. But a rifle-bullet, even when fired blindly, always seemed purposely aimed. And whereas we could usually hear a shell approaching, and take some sort of cover, the rifle-bullet gave no warning. So, though we learned not to duck a rifle-bullet because, once heard, it must have passed, it gave us a worse feeling of danger. Rifle-bullets in the open went hissing into the grass without much noise, but when we were in a trench, the bullets made a tremendous crack as they went over the hollow. Bullets often struck the barbed wire in front of the trenches, which sent them spinning with a head-over-heels motion—ping! rockety-ockety-ockety-ockety into the woods behind.

At battalion headquarters, a dug-out in the reserve line, about a quarter of a mile behind the front companies, the colonel, a twice-wounded regular, shook hands with us and offered us the whisky-bottle. He hoped that we would soon grow to like the regiment as much as our own. The sector had not long before been taken over from a French territorial division of men in the forties, who had a local Armistice with the Germans opposite—no firing, and apparently even civilian traffic allowed through the lines. So this dug-out happened to be unusually comfortable, with an ornamental lamp, a clean cloth, and polished silver on the table. The colonel, adjutant, doctor, second-in-command, and signalling officer had just finished dinner: it was civilized cooking—fresh meat and vegetables. Pictures pasted on the papered walls; spring-mattressed beds, a gramophone, easy chairs: we found it hard to reconcile these with the accounts we had read of troops standing waist-deep in mud, and gnawing a biscuit while shells burst all around. The adjutant posted us to our companies. 'Captain Dunn of "C" is your company commander,' he told me. 'The soundest officer in the battalion. By the way, remind him that I want him to send in that list of D.C.M. recommendations for the last show at once; but not more than two names, or else they won't give us any. Four is about the ration for any battalion in a dud show.'

Our guide took us up to the front line. We passed a group of men huddled over a brazier—small men, daubed with mud, talking quietly together in Welsh. They were wearing water-proof capes, for it had now started to rain, and cap-comforters, because the weather was cold for May. Although they could see we were officers, they did not jump to their feet and salute. I thought that this must be a convention of the trenches; and indeed it is laid down somewhere in the military text-books that the courtesy of the salute must be dispensed with in battle. But no, it was just slackness. We overtook a fatigue-party struggling up the trench loaded with timber lengths and bundles of sandbags, cursing plaintively as they slipped into sump-holes or entangled their burdens in the telephone wires. Fatigue-parties were always encumbered by their rifles and equipment, which it was a crime ever to have out of reach. After squeezing past this party, we had to stand aside to let a stretcher-case pass. 'Who's the poor devil, Dai?' the guide asked the leading stretcher-bearer. 'Sergeant Gallagher,' Dai answered. 'He thought he saw a Fritz in no-man's-land near our wire, so the silly booger takes one of them new issue percussion bombs and shoots it at 'im. Silly booger aims too low, it hits the top of the parapet and bursts back. Deoul! man, it breaks his silly blanking jaw and blows a great lump from his silly blanking face, whatever. Poor silly booger! Not worth sweating to get him back! He's put paid to, whatever.' The wounded man had a sandbag over his face. He died before they got him to the dressing-station.

I felt tired out by the time I reached company headquarters, sweating under a pack-valise like the men, and with all the usual furnishings hung at my belt—revolver, field-glasses, compass, whisky-flask, wire-cutters, periscope, and a lot more. A 'Christmas-tree' that was called. Those were the days in which officers had their swords sharpened by the armourer before sailing to France. I had been advised to leave mine back in the quartermaster-sergeants' billet, and never saw it again, or bothered about it. My hands were sticky with the clay from the side of the trench, and my legs soaked up to the calves. At 'C' Company headquarters, a two-roomed timber-built shelter in the side of a trench connecting the front and support lines, I found tablecloth and lamp again, whisky-bottle and glasses, shelves with books and magazines, and bunks in the next room. I reported to the company commander.

I had expected a grizzled veteran with a breastful of medals; but Dunn was actually two months younger than myself—

one of the fellowship of 'only survivors'. Captain Miller of the Black Watch in the same division was another. Miller had escaped from the Rue du Bois massacre by swimming down a flooded trench. Only survivors had great reputations. Miller used to be pointed at in the streets when the battalion was back in reserve billets. 'See that fellow? That's Jock Miller. Out from the start and hasn't got it yet.' Dunn did not let the war affect his morale at all. He greeted me very easily with: 'Well, what's the news from England? Oh, sorry, first I must introduce you. This is Walker—clever chap from Cambridge, fancies himself as an athlete. This is Jenkins, one of those elder patriots who chucked up their jobs to come here. This is Price —joined us yesterday, but we liked him at once: he brought some good whisky with him. Well, how long is the war going to last, and who's winning? We don't know a thing out here.' I told them about the war, and asked them about the trenches.

'About trenches,' said Dunn. 'Well, we don't know as much about trenches as the French do, and not near as much as Fritz does. We can't expect Fritz to help, but the French might do something. They are too greedy to let us have the benefit of their inventions. What wouldn't we give for their parachute-lights and aerial torpedoes! But there's never any connexion between the two armies, unless a battle is on, and then we generally let each other down.

'When I came out here first, all we did in trenches was to paddle about like ducks and use our rifles. We didn't think of them as places to live in, they were just temporary inconveniences. Now we work here all the time, not only for safety but for health. Night and day. First, at fire-steps, then at building traverses, improving the communication trenches, and so on; last comes our personal comfort—shelters and dug-outs. The territorial battalion that used to relieve us were hopeless. They used to sit down in the trench and say: "Oh, my God, this is the limit." Then they'd pull out pencil and paper and write home about it. Did no work on the traverses

52

or on fire positions. Consequence—they lost half their men from frost-bite and rheumatism, and one day the Germans broke in and scuppered a lot more of them. They'd allowed the work we'd done in the trench to go to ruin, and left the whole place like a sewage farm for us to take over again. We got sick as muck, and reported them several times to brigade headquarters; but they never improved. Slack officers, of course. Well, they got smashed, as I say, and were sent away to be lines-of-communication troops. Now we work with the First South Wales Borderers. They're all right. Awful swine, those territorials. Usen't to trouble about latrines at all; left food about to encourage rats; never filled a sandbag. I only once saw a job of work that they did: a steel loop-hole for sniping. But they put it facing square to the front, and quite unmasked, so two men got killed at it—absolute death-trap. Our chaps are all right, but not as right as they ought to be. The survivors of the show ten days ago are feeling pretty low, and the big new draft doesn't know a thing yet.'

'Listen,' said Walker, 'there's too much firing going on. The men have got the wind up over something. If Fritz thinks we're jumpy, he'll give us an extra bad time. I'll go up and stop them.'

Dunn went on: 'These Welshmen are peculiar. They won't stand being shouted at. They'll do anything if you explain the reason for it—do and die, but they have to know their reason why. The best way to make them behave is not to give them too much time to think. Work them off their feet. They are good workmen, too. But officers must work with them, not only direct the work. Our time-table is: breakfast at eight o'clock in the morning, clean trenches and inspect rifles, work all morning; lunch at twelve, work again from one till about six, when the men feed again. "Stand-to" at dusk for about an hour, work all night, "stand-to" for an hour before dawn. That's the general programme. Then there's sentry-duty. The men do two-hour sentry spells, then work two hours, then sleep two hours. At night, sentries are doubled, so working parties are smaller. We officers are on duty all day, and divide up the night into three-hourly watches.' He looked at his wristwatch. 'By the way,' he said, 'that carrying-party must have brought up the R.E. stuff by now. Time we all got to work. Look here, Graves, you lie down and have a doss on that bunk. I want you to take the watch before "stand-to". I'll wake you up and show you around. Where the hell's my revolver? I don't like to go out without it. Hello, Walker, what was wrong?'

Walker laughed. 'A chap from the new draft. He had never fired his musketry course at Cardiff, and tonight he fired ball for the first time. It went to his head. He'd had a brother killed up at Ypres, and sworn to avenge him. So he blazed off all his own ammunition at nothing, and two bandoliers out of the ammunition-box besides. They call him the "Human Maxim" now. His foresight's misty with heat. Corporal Parry should have stopped him; but he just leant up against the traverse and shrieked with laughter. I gave them both a good cursing. Some other new chaps started blazing away too. Fritz retaliated with machine-guns and whizz-bangs. No casualties. I don't know why. It's all quiet now. Everybody ready?'

When they went off, I rolled up in my blanket and fell asleep. Dunn woke me at about one o'clock. 'Your watch,' he said. I jumped out of the bunk with a rustle of straw; my feet were sore and clammy in my boots. I was cold, too. 'Here's the rocket-pistol and a few flares. Not a bad night. It's stopped raining. Put your equipment on over your raincoat, or you won't be able to get at your revolver. Got a torch? Good. About this flare business. Don't use the pistol too much. We haven't many flares, and if there's an attack we'll need as many as we can get. But use it if you think something's doing. Fritz is always sending up flare-lights; he's got as many as he wants.'

Dunn showed me around the line. The battalion frontage was about eight hundred yards. Each company held some two hundred of these, with two platoons in the front line, and two in the support line about a hundred yards back. He introduced me to the platoon sergeants, more particularly to Sergeant Eastmond and told him to give me any information I wanted; then went back to sleep, asking to be woken at once if anything went wrong. I found myself in charge of the line. Sergeant Eastmond being busy with a working-party, I went round by myself. The men of the working-party, whose job was to repair the traverses, or safety-buttresses, of the trench, looked curiously at me. They were filling sandbags with earth, piling them up bricklayer fashion, the headers and stretchers alternating, then patting them flat with spades. The sentries stood on the fire-step at the corners of the traverses, stamping their feet and blowing on their fingers. Every now and then they peered over the top for a few seconds. Two parties, each of an N.C.O. and two men, were out in the company listening-posts, connected with the front trench by a sap about fifty yards long. The German front line stretched some three hundred yards beyond. From berths hollowed in the sides of the trench and curtained with sandbags came the grunt of sleeping men.

I jumped up on the fire-step beside the sentry and cautiously raised my head, staring over the parapet. I could see nothing except the wooden pickets supporting our protecting barbed-wire entanglements, and a dark patch or two of bushes beyond. The darkness seemed to move and shake about as I looked at it; the bushes started travelling, singly at first, then both together. The pickets did the same. I was glad of the sentry beside me; he gave his name as Beaumont. 'They're quiet tonight, sir,' he said. 'A relief going on; I think so, surely.'

I said: 'It's funny how those bushes seem to move.'

'Aye, they do play queer tricks. Is this your first spell in trenches, sir?'

A German flare shot up, broke into bright flame, dropped slowly and went hissing into the grass just behind our trench, showing up the bushes and pickets. Instinctively I moved.

'It's bad to do that, sir,' he said, as a rifle-bullet cracked and seemed to pass right between us. 'Keep still, sir, and they can't spot you. Not but what a flare is a bad thing to fall on you. I've seen them burn a hole in a man.'

I spent the rest of my watch in acquainting myself with the geography of the trench-section, finding how easy it was to get lost among *culs-de-sac* and disused alleys. Twice I overshot the company frontage and wandered among the Munster Fusiliers on the left. Once I tripped and fell with a splash into deep mud. My watch ended when the first signs of dawn showed. I passed the word along the line for the company to stand-to arms. The N.C.O.s whispered hoarsely into the dug-outs, 'Stand-to, stand-to', and out the men tumbled with their rifles in their hands. Going towards company head-quarters to wake the officers I saw a man lying on his face in a machine-gun shelter. I stopped and said: 'Stand-to, there!' I flashed my torch on him and saw that one of his feet was bare.

The machine-gunner beside him said: 'No good talking to him, sir.'

I asked: 'What's wrong? Why has he taken his boot and sock off?'

'Look for yourself, sir!'

I shook the sleeper by the arm and noticed suddenly the hole in the back of his head. He had taken off the boot and sock to pull the trigger of his rifle with one toe; the muzzle was in his mouth.

'Why did he do it?' I asked.

'He went through the last push, sir, and that sent him a bit queer; on top of that he got bad news from Limerick about his girl and another chap.'

He belonged to the Munsters—their machine-guns

overlapped the left of our company—and his suicide had already been reported. Two Irish officers came up. 'We've had several of these lately,' one of them told me. Then he said to the other. 'While I remember, Callaghan, don't forget to write to his next-of-kin. Usual sort of letter; tell them he died a soldier's death, anything you like. I'm not going to report it as suicide.'

At stand-to, rum and tea were served out. I looked at the German trenches through a periscope—a distant streak of sandbags. The enemy gave no sign, except for a wisp or two of wood-smoke where they, too. were boiling up a hot drink. Between us and them lay a flat meadow with cornflowers, marguerites and poppies growing in the long grass, a few shell-holes, the bushes I had seen the night before, the wreck of an aeroplane, our barbed wire and theirs. Three-quarters of a mile away stood a big ruined house; a quarter of a mile behind that, a red-brick village—Auchy—poplars and hay-stacks, a tall chimney, and another village—Haisnes. Half-right, pit-head and smaller slag-heaps. La Bassée lay half-left; the sun caught the weather-vane of the church and made it twinkle.

In the interval between stand-to and breakfast, the men who were not getting in a bit of extra sleep sat about talking and smoking, writing letters home, cleaning their rifles, running their thumbnails up the seams of their shirts to kill lice, gambling. Lice were a standing joke. Young Bumford handed me one: 'We was just having an argument as to whether it's best to kill the old ones or the young ones, sir. Morgan here says that if you kill the old ones, the young ones die of grief; but Parry here, sir, he says that the young ones are easier to kill and you can catch the old ones when they go to the funeral.' He appealed to me as an arbiter: 'You've been to college, sir, haven't you?'

I said: 'Yes, I have, but so had Crawshay Bailey's brother Norwich.'

The platoon treasured this as a wonderfully witty answer. *Crawshay Bailey* is one of the idiotic songs of Wales. Crawshay Bailey himself 'had an engine and he couldn't make it go', and all his relatives in the song had similar shortcomings. Crawshay Bailey's brother Norwich, for instance, was fond of oatmeal porridge, but was sent to Cardiff College, for to get a bit of knowledge. After that, I had no trouble with the platoon.

Breakfast at company headquarters consisted of bacon, eggs, coffee, toast and marmalade. There were three chairs and two ammunition-boxes to sit on. Accustomed to company commanders who never took junior officers into their confidence, I liked the way that questions of the moment were settled at meal-times by a sort of board-meeting with Dunn as chairman. On this first morning we had a long debate on how to keep sentries awake. Dunn finally issued a company order forbidding them to lean against traverses; it made them sleepy. Besides, when they fired, the flash would come always from the same place. The Germans might fix a rifle on the spot after a time. I told Dunn of the bullet that passed between Beaumont and myself.

'Sounds like a fixed rifle,' he said, 'because not one aimed shot in a hundred comes as close as that at night. And we had a chap killed in that very traverse the night we came in.' The Bavarian Guards Reserve, who were opposite us at the time, seemed to have complete control of the sniping situation.

Dunn gave me the characters of the N.C.O.s in my platoon: which were trustworthy and which had to be watched. He had begun telling me just how much I could expect from the men at my platoon inspection of rifles and equipment, when a soldier came rushing in, his eyes blank with horror and excitement. 'Gas, sir, gas! They're using gas!'

'My God!' exclaimed Price. We all looked at Dunn, whose soldier-servant the man was.

Dunn said imperturbably: 'Very well, Kingdom, bring me

my respirator from the other room, and another pot of marma-lade.'

The alarm had originated with smoke blowing across from the German trenches, where breakfast must also have been in progress; we knew the German meal-times by a slackening down of rifle-fire. Gas had become a nightmare. Nobody believed in the efficacy of our respirators, though advertised as proof against any gas the enemy could send over. Pink forms marked 'Urgent' constantly arrived from headquarters to explain how to use these accessories: all contradictory. First, the respirators were to be kept soaking wet, then they were to be kept dry, then they were to be worn in a satchel, then, again, the satchel was not to be used.

9

HERE are extracts from letters that I wrote at this time. I have restored the names of places, which we were forbidden to mention:

May 21st, 1915. Back in billets again at a coal-mining village called La Bourse. It is not more than three miles and a half from the front line, but the miners are still working. As we came out of the trenches the Germans were shelling the wood by Cambrin village, searching for one of our batteries. I don't think they got it, but it was fun to see the poplar-trees being lopped down like tulips when the whizz-bangs hit them square. As we marched down the *pavé* road from Cambrin, the men straggled along out of step and out of fours. Their feet were sore from having had their boots on for a week— they have only one spare pair of socks issued to them. Well, anyhow, marching on cobbled roads is difficult, so when a staff-officer came by in a Rolls-Royce and cursed us for bad march-discipline, I felt like throwing something at him. Trench soldiers hate the staff and the staff know it. The principal disagreement seems to be about the extent to which trench conditions should modify discipline.

May 22nd. A colossal bombardment by the French at Souchez, a few miles away—continuous roar of artillery, coloured flares, shells bursting all along the ridge by Notre Dame de Lorette. I couldn't sleep. The noise went on all night. Instead of dying away it grew and grew, till the whole air rocked and shook; the sky was lit up with huge flashes. I lay in my feather bed and sweated.

May 23rd. Two young miners, in another company, disliked their sergeant, who had a down on them and gave them all the most dirty and dangerous jobs. When they were in billets he crimed them for things they hadn't done; so they decided to kill him. Later, they reported at Battalion Orderly Room and asked to see the adjutant. This was irregular, because a private is forbidden to address an officer without an N.C.O. of his own company acting as go-between. The adjutant happened to see them and asked: 'Well, what is it you want?'

Smartly slapping the small-of-the-butt of their sloped rifles, they said: 'We've come to report, sir, that we're very sorry, but we've shot our company sergeant-major.'

The adjutant said: 'Good heavens, how did that happen?'

'It was an accident, sir.'

'What do you mean, you damn fools? Did you mistake him for a spy?'

'No, sir, we mistook him for our platoon sergeant.'

So they were both court-martialled and shot by a firing-squad of their own company against the wall of a convent at Béthune. Their last words were the battalion rallying-cry: 'Stick it, the Welch!' (They say that a certain Captain Haggard first used it in the battle of Ypres when he was mortally wounded.) The French military governor was present at the execution, and made a little speech saying how gloriously British soldiers can die.

You'd be surprised at the amount of waste that goes on in the trenches. Ration biscuits are in general use as fuel for boiling up dixies, because kindling is scarce. Our machine-gun crew boil their hot water by firing off belt after belt of ammunition at no particular target, just generally spraying the German line. After several pounds' worth of ammunition has been used, the water in the guns—which are water-cooled—begins to boil. They say they make German ration- and carrying-parties behind the line pay for their early-morning cup of tea. But the real charge will be on income-tax after the war.

May 28th. In trenches among the Cuinchy brick-stacks. Not my idea of trenches. There has been a lot of fighting hereabouts. The trenches have made themselves rather than been made, and run inconsequently in and out of the big thirty-foot high stacks of bricks; it is most confusing. The parapet of a trench which we don't occupy is built up with ammunition-boxes and corpses. Everything here is wet and smelly. The Germans are very close: they have half the brick-stacks, we have the other half. Each side snipes down from the top of its brick-stacks into the other's trenches. This is also a great place for German rifle-grenades and trench-mortars. We can't reply properly; we have only a meagre supply of rifle-grenades and nothing to equal the German sausage mortar-bomb. This morning about breakfast-time, just as I came out of my dug-out, a rifle-grenade landed within six feet of me. For some reason, instead of falling on its head and exploding, it landed with its stick in the wet clay and stood there looking at me. They are difficult to see coming; they are shot from a rifle, with its butt on the ground, tilted, and go up a long way before turning over and coming down head-first. I can't understand why this particular rifle-grenade fell as it did; the chances were impossibly against it.

'Sausages' are easy to see and dodge, but they make a terrible noise when they drop. We have had about ten casualties in our company today from them. I find that my reactions to danger are extraordinarily quick; but everyone gets like that. We can sort out all the different explosions and disregard whichever don't concern us—such as the artillery duel, machine-gun-fire at the next company to us, desultory rifle-fire. But we pick out at once the faint plop! of the mortar that sends off a sausage, or the muffled rifle noise when a grenade is fired. The men are much afraid, yet always joking. The company sergeant-major stands behind Number Eleven brick-stack and shoots at sausages with a rifle as they come over; trying to explode them in the air. He says that it's better than pigeon-shooting. He hasn't hit one yet.

Last night a lot of German stuff was flying about, including shrapnel. I heard one shell whish-whishing towards me and dropped flat. It burst just over the trench where 'Petticoat Lane' runs into 'Lowndes Square'. My ears sang as though there were gnats in them, and a bright scarlet light shone over everything. My shoulder got twisted in falling and I thought I had been hit, but I hadn't been. The vibration made my chest sing, too, in a curious way, and I lost my sense of equilibrium. I was ashamed when the sergeant-major came along the trench and found me on all fours, still unable to stand up straight.

June 9th. Beaumont, of whom I told you in my last letter, also got killed—the last unwounded survivor of the original battalion, except for the transport men. Everyone was swearing angrily, but an R.E. officer came up and told me that he had a tunnel driven under the German front line, and that if my chaps wanted to do a bit of bombing, now was the time. So he sent the mine up—it was not a big one, he said, but it made a tremendous noise and covered us with dirt—and we waited for a few seconds for the other Germans to rush up to help the wounded away, and then chucked all the bombs we had.

Beaumont had been telling me how he had won about five pounds' worth of francs in the sweepstake after the Rue du Bois show: a sweepstake of the sort that leaves no bitterness behind it. Before a show, the platoon pools all its available cash and the survivors divide it up afterwards. Those who are killed can't complain, the wounded would have given far more than that to escape as they have, and the unwounded regard the money as a consolation prize for still being here.

June 24th. We are billeted in the cellars of Vermelles, which was taken and retaken eight times last October. We came up two nights ago. Next morning we found the deserted gardens of the town very pleasant to walk about in; they are quite overgrown and flowers have seeded themselves about wildly. One garden has currant bushes in it. I and the company sergeant-major started eating along the line from opposite ends without noticing each other. When we did, we both remembered our dignity, he as a company sergeant-major, and I as an officer. He saluted, I acknowledged the salute, we both walked away. A minute or two later, we both came back hoping that the coast was clear and again, after an exchange of salutes, had to leave the currants and pretend that we were merely admiring the flowers. I don't quite know why I behaved like that. The C.S.M. is a regular, and therefore obliged to stop eating in the presence of an officer. So, I suppose, courtesy to his scruples made me stop too. Anyhow, along came a couple of privates and stripped the bushes clean.

This afternoon we had a cricket match, officers *versus* sergeants, in an enclosure between some houses out of observation from the enemy. Our front line is perhaps three-quarters of a mile away. I made top score, twenty-four; the bat was a bit of a rafter; the ball, a piece of rag tied round with string; and the wicket, a parrot-cage with the clean, dry corpse of a parrot inside. It had evidently died when the French evacuated the town.

Machine-gun-fire broke up the match. It was not aimed at us; the Germans were shooting at one of our aeroplanes, and the bullets falling from a great height had a penetrative power greater than an ordinary spent bullet.

This is a very idle life, except for night-digging on the reserve line. We can't drill because we are too near the Germans, and no fortification needs doing in the village. Today two spies were shot: a civilian who had hung on in a cellar and was, apparently, flashing news to the Germans; and a German soldier disguised as an R.E. corporal; found tampering with the telephone wires. We officers spend a lot of time revolver-shooting. Jenkins brought out a beautiful target from the only undestroyed living-room in our billet-area: a glass case full of artificial fruit and flowers. We put it up on a post at fifty yards' range. He said: 'I've always wanted to smash one of these damn objects. My aunt has one. It's the sort of thing that *would* survive an intense bombardment.' I smothered a tender impulse to rescue it. So we have five shots each, in turn. Everyone missed. Then we went up to within twenty yards and fired a volley. Someone hit the post and knocked the case off into the grass. Jenkins said: 'Drat the thing; it must be bewitched. Let's take it back.' The glass was unbroken, but some of the fruit had come loose. Walker said: 'No, it's in pain. We must put it out of its suffering.' He gave it the *coup de grâce* from close quarters.

10

WITH the advance of summer came new types of bombs and trench-mortars, heavier shelling, improved gas-masks and a general tightening-up of discipline. We met the first battalions of the New Army, and felt like scarecrows by comparison. Our battalion went in and out of the Cambrin and Cuinchy trenches, with billets in Béthune and the neighbouring villages. By this time I had caught the pessimism of the First Division. Its spirit in the trenches was largely defensive; the policy being not to stir the Germans into more than their usual hostility.

Constant mining went on in the Cambrin–Cuinchy sector. We had the prospect of being blown up at any moment. An officer of the R.E. tunnelling company won the Victoria Cross while we were there. A duel of mining and counter-mining had been going on. When the Germans began to undermine his original boring, he rapidly tunnelled beneath them. It was touch and go who would get ready first. He won. But when he detonated his mine from the trench by an electric lead, nothing happened. So he ran down again, retamped the charge, and got back just in time to set it off before the Germans fired theirs. I had visited the upper boring on the previous day. It ran about twenty feet under the German lines. At the end of the gallery I found a Welsh miner on listening duty, one of our own battalion, who had transferred to the Royal Engineers. He cautioned me to silence. I could distinctly hear the Germans working somewhere below us. He whispered: 'So long as they work, I don't mind. It's when they blinking stop!' He did his two-hour spell by candle-light in the cramped and stuffy dead-end, reading a book. The mining officer had told me that the men were allowed to read; it didn't interfere with their listening. The book was a paper-backed novelette called *From Mill Girl to Duchess*. The tunnelling companies were notorious thieves, by the way. They would snatch things up from the trench and scurry off with them into their borings; just like mice.

At the end of July, Robertson, one of the other Royal Welch officers attached to the Welsh, and myself had orders to proceed to the Laventie sector. We were to report to the Second Battalion of the Royal Welch Fusiliers. When we eventually arrived we saluted the adjutant smartly, gave our names, and told him that we were Third Battalion officers posted to the regiment. He did not shake hands with us, offer us a drink, or say a word of welcome. 'I see,' he said coldly. 'Well, which of you is senior? Oh, never mind. Give your particulars to the R.S.M. Tell him to post whoever is senior to "A" Company and the other to "B" Company.'

The regimental sergeant-major took our particulars and introduced me to Hilary Drake-Brockman, a young second-lieutenant of 'A' Company, to which I had been posted. He was a special reservist of the East Surrey Regiment, and contemptuously known as 'the Surrey-man'. He took me along to the company billet. When out of earshot of battalion headquarters, I asked him: 'What's wrong with the adjutant? Why didn't he shake hands or give me any sort of decent welcome?'

The Surrey-man said: 'Well, it's your regiment, not mine. They're all like that here. You must realize that this is one of the only four regular battalions in France that has remained still more or less its old self. This is the Nineteenth Brigade, the luckiest in France. It hasn't been permanently attached to any division, but gets used as army reserve, to put in wherever one has been badly knocked. So, except for the Retreat, where it lost about a company, and Fromelles, where it lost half of what was left, it's been practically undamaged. More than two hundred of the wounded have rejoined since. All our company commanders are regulars, and so are all our N.C.O.s. The peacetime custom of taking no notice of newly-joined officers is still more or less kept up for the first six months. The senior officers are beasts. If you open your mouth or make the slightest noise in the mess, they jump down your throat. Only officers of the rank of captain are allowed to drink whisky or turn on the gramophone. We've got to jolly well keep still and look like furniture. It's just like peacetime.

'We've even got a polo-ground here. Subalterns who can't ride like angels have to attend riding-school every afternoon while we're in billets. They give us hell, too. Two of us have been at it for four months and haven't passed out yet. They keep us trotting round the field, with crossed stirrups most of the time. Yesterday we were called up suddenly without being given time to change into breeches. That reminds me, you notice everybody's wearing shorts? It's a regimental order. The battalion thinks it's still in India. It makes me laugh sometimes. The funny thing is that they don't realize how badly they're treating us—it's such an honour to be serving with the regiment. So better pretend you don't care what they do or say.'

I protested: 'But all this is childish. Is there a war on here, or isn't there?'

'The Royal Welch don't recognize it socially,' he answered. 'Still, in trenches I'd rather be with this battalion than with any other I have met. The senior officers do know their job, whatever else one may say about them, and the N.C.O.s are absolutely to be trusted, too.'

We went together into the big château near the church. About fifteen officers of various ranks were sitting in chairs reading the week's illustrated papers or, the seniors at least, talking quietly. At the door I said, 'Good morning, gentlemen', the new officer's customary greeting to the mess. No answer. Everybody glanced at me curiously. The silence that my entry had caused was soon broken by the gramophone, which began carolling:

> We've been married just one year,
> And Oh, we've got the sweetest,
> We've got the neatest,
> We've got the cutest
> Little oil-stove.

I found a chair in the background and picked up *The Field*. The door burst open suddenly, and a lieutenant-colonel with a red face and angry eye burst in. 'Who the blazes put that record on?' he shouted to the mess. 'One of the bloody warts, I expect. Take it off, somebody! It makes me sick. Let's have some real music. Put on the "Angelus".'

Two subalterns (in the Royal Welch a subaltern had to answer to the name of 'wart') sprang up, stopped the gramophone, and put on 'When the Angelus is ringing'. The young captain who had put on 'We've been married' shrugged his shoulders and went on reading; the other faces in the room remained blank.

'Who's that?' I whispered to the Surrey-man.

He frowned. 'That's Buzz Off,' he muttered, 'the second-in-command.'

Before the record had finished, the door opened and in came the colonel; Buzz Off reappeared with him. Everybody jumped up and said in unison, 'Good morning, sir', this being his first appearance that day.

Instead of returning our loyal greeting and asking us to sit down, he turned spitefully to the gramophone: 'Who on earth puts this wretched "Angelus" on every time I come into the mess? For heaven's sake play something cheery for a change!' With his own hands he took off the 'Angelus', wound up the gramophone and put on 'We've been married just one year'. At that moment a gong rang for lunch, and he abandoned his task.

We filed into the next room, a ball-room with mirrors and a decorated ceiling, and took our places at a long, polished table. The seniors sat at the top, the juniors competed for seats as far away from them as possible. Unluckily I got a seat at the foot of the table, facing the colonel, the adjutant and Buzz Off. Not a word was spoken down my end, except an occasional whisper for the salt or the beer. Robertson, who had not been warned, asked the mess waiter for whisky. 'Sorry, sir,' said the mess waiter, 'it's against orders for the young officers.' Robertson was a man of forty-two, a solicitor with a large practice, and had stood for Parliament in the Yarmouth division at the previous election.

I saw Buzz Off glaring at us and busied myself with my meat and potatoes.

He nudged the adjutant. 'Who are those two funny ones down there, Charley?' he asked.

'New this morning from the militia. Answer to the names of Robertson and Graves.'

'Which is which?' asked the colonel.

'I'm Robertson, sir.'

'I wasn't asking you.'

Robertson winced but said nothing. Then Buzz Off noticed something.

'T'other wart's wearing a wind-up tunic.' Then he bent forward and asked me loudly: 'You there, wart! Why the hell are you wearing your stars on your shoulder instead of your sleeve?'

My mouth was full, and everybody had his eyes on me. I swallowed the lump of meat whole and said: 'Shoulder stars were a regimental order in the Welsh Regiment, sir. I understood that it was the same everywhere in France.'

The colonel turned puzzled to the adjutant: 'Why on earth is the man talking about the Welsh Regiment?' And then to me: 'As soon as you have finished your lunch you will visit the master-tailor. Report at the Orderly Room when you're properly dressed.'

In a severe struggle between resentment and regimental loyalty, resentment for the moment had the better of it. I said under my breath: 'You damned snobs! I'll survive you all. There'll come a time when there won't be one of you left in the battalion to remember this mess at Laventie.'

We went up to the trenches that night. They were 'high-command' trenches—because water was struck whenever one dug down three feet, the parapet and parados had been built up man-high. I found my platoon curt and reserved. Even on sentry-duty at night my men would never talk confidentially about themselves and their families, like my platoon in the Welsh Regiment.

My first night, Captain Thomas, my company commander, asked whether I would like to go out on patrol. It was the regimental custom to test new officers in this way, and none dared excuse himself. Both battalions of the Royal Welch Fusiliers had made it a point of honour to dominate no-man's-land from dusk to dawn. There was never a night at Laventie when a message did not come down the line from sentry to sentry: 'Pass the word; officer's patrol going out.' My orders for this patrol were to see whether a certain German sap-head was occupied by night or not.

The platoon-sergeant, Sergeant Townsend, and I went out from the trenches at about ten o'clock, both carrying revolvers. We had pulled socks, with the toes cut off, over our bare knees, to prevent them showing up in the dark and to make crawling easier. We went ten yards at a time, slowly, not on all fours, but wriggling flat along the ground. After each movement we lay and watched for about ten minutes. We crawled through our own wire entanglements and along a dry ditch; ripping our clothes on more barbed-wire, glaring into the darkness until it began turning round and round. Once I snatched my fingers in horror from where I had planted them on the slimy body of an old corpse. We nudged each other with rapidly beating hearts at the slightest noise or suspicion: crawling, watching, crawling, shamming dead under the blinding light of enemy flares, and again crawling, watching, crawling. A Second Battalion officer, who revisited these Laventie trenches after the war ended told me the other day of the ridiculously small area of no-man's-land compared with its seeming immensity on the long, painful journeys that he had made over it.

We found the gap in the German wire and at last came within five yards of the sap-head. We waited twenty minutes, listening for any signs of its occupation. Then I nudged Sergeant Townsend and, revolver in hand, we wriggled quickly forward and slid into it. It was about three feet deep and unoccupied. On the floor were a few empty cartridges, and a wicker basket containing something large and smooth and round, twice the size of a football. Very, very carefully I groped and felt all around it in the dark. I was afraid that it might be some sort of infernal machine. Eventually I dared lift it out and carry it back, suspecting that it might be one of the German gas-cylinders we had heard so much about.

We got home after making a journey of perhaps two hundred yards in rather more than two hours. The sentries passed along the word that we were in again. Our prize proved to be a large glass container quarter-filled with some pale yellow liquid. This was sent down to battalion head-quarters, and from there to the divisional intelligence officer. Everybody seemed greatly interested in it. The theory was that the vessel contained a chemical for re-damping gas-masks, though it may well have been dregs of country wine mixed with rain water. I never heard the official report. The colonel, however, told Captain Thomas in the hearing of the Surrey-man: 'Your new wart seems to have more guts than the others.'

After this I went on patrol fairly often, finding that the only thing respected in young officers was personal courage. Besides, I had cannily worked it out like this. My best way of lasting through to the end of the war would be to get wounded. The best time to get wounded would be at night and in the open, with rifle-fire more or less unaimed and my whole body exposed. Best, also, to get wounded when there was no rush on the dressing-station services, and while the back areas were not being heavily shelled. Best to get wounded, therefore, on a night patrol in a quiet sector. One could usually manage to crawl into a shell-hole until help arrived.

Still, patrolling had its peculiar risks. If a German patrol found a wounded man, they were as likely as not to cut his throat. The bowie-knife was a favourite German patrol weapon because of its silence. (We inclined more to the 'cosh', a loaded stick.) The most important information that a patrol could bring back was to what regiment and division the troops opposite belonged. So if it were impossible to get a wounded enemy back without danger to oneself, he had to be stripped of his badges. To do that quickly and silently, it might be necessary first to cut his throat or beat in his skull.

Sir Pyers Mostyn, a Royal Welch lieutenant who often went out patrolling at Laventie, had a feud with a German patrol on the left of the battalion frontage. Our patrols usually consisted of an officer and one, or at the most, two men; German patrols, of six or seven men under an N.C.O. German officers did not, as one of our sergeant-majors put it, believe in 'keeping a dog and barking themselves'; so they left as much as they decently could to their N.C.O.s. One night Mostyn caught sight of his opponents; he had raised himself on his knees to throw a percussion bomb, when they fired and wounded him in the arm, which immediately went numb. He caught the bomb before it hit the ground, threw it at them with his left hand, and in the confusion that followed got back to the trench.

The Second Royal Welch, unlike the Second Welsh, believed themselves better trench fighters than the Germans. With the Second Welsh it was not cowardice but modesty. With the Second Royal Welch it was not vainglory but courage: as soon as they arrived in a new sector they insisted on getting fire ascendancy. Having found out, from the troops whom they relieved, all possible information as to enemy snipers, machine-guns, and patrols, they set themselves to deal with them one by one. Machine-guns first. As soon as a machine-gun started traversing down a trench by night, the whole platoon farthest removed from its fire would open five rounds rapid at it. The machine-gun would usually stop suddenly, but start again after a minute or two. Again five rounds rapid. Then it gave up.

When the enemy machine-guns had been discouraged, our patrols would go out with bombs to claim possession of no-man's-land. At dawn next morning came the struggle for sniping ascendancy. The Germans had special regimental snipers, trained in camouflaging themselves. I saw one killed once at Cuinchy, who had been firing all day from a shell-hole between the lines. He wore a sort of cape made of imitation grass, his face was painted green and brown, and his rifle was also green-fringed. A number of empty cartridges lay beside him, and his cap bore the special oak-leaf badge. Few of our battalions attempted to get control of the sniping situation. The Germans had the advantage of having many times more telescopic sights than we did, and bullet-proof steel loop-holes. Also a system by which snipers were kept for months in the same sector until they knew all the loop-holes and shallow places in our trenches, and the tracks that our ration-parties used above-ground by night, and where our traverses occurred, and so on, better than most of us did ourselves.

British snipers changed their trenches, with their battalions, every week or two, and never had time to study the German trench geography. But at least we counted on getting rid of the unprofessional sniper. Later we secured an elephant-gun that could send a bullet through enemy loop-holes; and if we failed to locate the loop-hole of a persistent sniper, we tried to dislodge him with a volley of rifle-grenades, or even by ringing up the artillery.

There was one advantage of which no progress or retreat of the enemy could rob us, namely that we always more or less faced east. Dawn broke behind the German lines, and they did not realize that for several minutes every morning we could see them, while still invisible ourselves. German night wiring-parties often stayed out too long, and we could get a man or two as they went back.

I had been with the Royal Welch about three weeks, when the Nineteenth Brigade moved south. The first trenches we went into on arrival were the Cuinchy brick-stacks. My company held the canal-bank frontage, a few hundred yards to the left of where I had been with the Welsh Regiment at the end of May. The colonel called for a patrol to visit the side of the tow-path, where we had heard suspicious sounds, and see whether they came from a working-party. I volunteered to go at dark. But that night the moon shone so bright and full that it dazzled the eyes. Between us and the Germans lay a flat stretch of about two hundred yards, broken only by shell-craters and an occasional patch of coarse grass. I was not with my own company, but lent to 'B', which had two officers away on leave. The company commander asked: 'You're not going out on patrol tonight, Graves, are you? It's almost as bright as day.'

'All the more reason for going,' I answered. 'They won't be expecting me. Will you please keep everything as usual? Let the men fire an occasional rifle, and send up a flare every half-hour. If I go carefully, the Germans won't see me.'

While we were having supper, I nervously knocked over a cup of tea, and after that a plate. Freeman, the company commander, said: 'Look here, I'll phone through to battalion and tell them it's too bright for your patrol.' But I knew that, if he did, Buzz Off would accuse me of cold feet.

So one Sergeant Williams and I put on our crawlers, and went out by way of a mine-crater at the side of the tow-path. We had no need to stare that night. We could see only too clearly. Our plan was to wait for an opportunity to move quickly, stop dead and trust to luck, then move on quickly again. We planned our rushes from shell-hole to shell-hole, the opportunities being provided by artillery or machine-gun-fire, which would distract the sentries. Many of the craters contained the corpses of men who had been wounded and crept in there to die. Some were skeletons, picked clean by the rats.

We got to within thirty yards of a big German working-party, who were digging a trench ahead of their front line. Between them and us we counted a covering-party of ten men lying on the grass in their greatcoats. We had gone far enough. A German lay on his back about twelve yards off, humming a tune. It was the 'Merry Widow' waltz. The sergeant, from behind me, pressed my foot with his hand and showed me the revolver he was carrying. He raised his eyebrows inquiringly. I signalled 'no'. We turned to go back, finding it hard not to move too quickly. We had got about half-way, when a German machine-gun opened traversing fire along the top of our trenches. We immediately jumped to our feet; the bullets were brushing the grass, so to stand up was safer. We walked the rest of the way home, but moving irregularly to distract the aim of the covering-party if they saw us. Back in the trench, I rang up brigade artillery, and asked for as much shrapnel as they could spare, fifty yards short of where the German front trench touched the tow-path; I knew that one of the night-lines of the battery supporting us was trained near enough to this point. A minute and a quarter later the shells starting coming over. Hearing the clash of downed tools and distant shouts and cries, we reckoned the probable casualties.

The next morning, at stand-to, Buzz Off came up to me: 'I hear you were on patrol last night?'

'Yes, sir.'

He asked for particulars. When I told him about the covering-party, he cursed me for not 'scuppering them with that revolver of yours'. As he turned away, he snorted 'Cold feet!'

11

By the end of August 1915, particulars of the coming offensive against La Bassée were beginning to leak through the young staff-officers. The French civilians knew about it; and so, naturally, did the Germans. Every night now new batteries and lorry-trains of shells came rumbling up the Béthune–La Bassée road. Other signs of movement included orders for the evacuation of hospitals; the appearance of cavalry and New Army divisions; issue of new types of weapons. Then Royal Engineer officers supervised the digging of pits at intervals along the front line. They were sworn not to reveal what these were for, but we knew that it would be gas-cylinders. Ladders for climbing quickly out of trenches were brought up by the lorry-load and dumped at Cambrin village. As early as September 3rd I had a bet with Robertson that our division would attack from the Cambrin–Cuinchy line.

On September 19th we relieved the Middlesex Regiment at Cambrin, and were told that these would be the trenches from which we attacked. The preliminary bombardment had already started, a week in advance. This was by far the heaviest bombardment from our own guns we had yet seen. The trenches shook properly, and a great cloud of drifting shell-smoke obscured the German lines. Shells went over our heads in a steady stream; we had to shout to make our neighbours hear. Dying down a little at night, the racket began again every morning at dawn, a little louder each time. The Germans retaliated, though not very vigorously. Most of their heavy artillery had been withdrawn from this sector, we were told, and sent across to the Russian front. More casualties came from our own shorts and blow-backs than from German shells. Much of the ammunition that our batteries were using came from the United States and contained a high percentage of duds; the driving bands were always coming off. We had fifty casualties in the ranks and three officer casualties, including Buzz Off—badly wounded in the head. This happened before steel helmets were issued; we would not have lost nearly so many with those.

On the morning of the 23rd, Thomas came back from battalion headquarters with orders for our company. I copied down the orders:

FIRST OBJECTIVE—*Les Briques Farm*—The big house plainly visible to our front, surrounded by trees. To get this it is necessary to cross three lines of enemy trenches. The first is three hundred yards distant, the second four hundred, and the third about six hundred. We then cross two railways. Behind the second railway line is a German trench called the Brick Trench. Then comes the Farm, a strong place with moat and cellars and a kitchen garden strongly staked and wired.

SECOND OBJECTIVE—*The Town of Auchy*—This is also plainly visible from our trenches. It is four hundred yards beyond the Farm and defended by two lines of trenches.

THIRD OBJECTIVE—*Village of Haisnes*—Conspicuous by high-spired church. Our eventual line will be taken up on the railway behind this village, where we will dig in and await reinforcements.

Thomas added: 'Between the six of us, but you youngsters must be careful not to let the men know, this is what they call a "subsidiary attack". There will be no troops in support. We've just got to go over and keep the enemy busy while the folk on our right do the real work. You notice that the bombardment is much heavier over there.' He went on:

The attack will be preceded by forty minutes' discharge of the accessory,* which will clear the path for a thousand yards, so that the two railway lines will be occupied without difficulty. Our advance will follow closely behind the accessory. Behind us are three fresh divisions and the Cavalry Corps. It is expected we shall have no difficulty in breaking through. All men will parade with their platoons; pioneers, servants, etc., to be warned. All platoons to be properly told off under N.C.O.s. Every N.C.O. is to know exactly what is expected of him, and when to take over command in case of casualties. Men who lose touch must join up with the nearest company or regiment and push on. Owing to the strength of the accessory, men should be warned against remaining too long in captured trenches where the accessory is likely to collect, but to keep to the open and above all to push on. It is important that if smoke-helmets have to be pulled down they must be tucked in under the shirt.

Thomas said: 'It's damnable. It's not soldiering to use stuff like that, even though the Germans did start it. It's dirty, and

* The gas-cylinders had by this time been put into position on the front line. A special order came round imposing severe penalties on anyone who used any word but 'accessory' in speaking of the gas. This was to keep it secret, but the French civilians knew all about the scheme long before this.

it'll bring us bad luck. We're sure to bungle it. Take those new gas-companies—sorry, excuse me this once, I mean accessory-companies—their very look makes me tremble. Chemistry-dons from London University, a few lads straight from school, one or two N.C.O.s of the old-soldier type, trained together for three weeks, then given a job as responsible as this. Of course they'll bungle it. How could they do anything else?'

That afternoon I repeated the whole rigmarole to the platoon, and told them of the inevitable success attending our assault. We spent the night repairing damaged trenches.

When morning came we were relieved by the Middlesex, and marched back to Béthune, where we dumped our spare kit. At that time the battalion officers messed together with the officers of a New Army division. The General Staff Officer of the New Army division, a staff-colonel, knew our adjutant well. They had played polo together in India. I happened to be sitting opposite them at a meal. The G.S.O. said, rather drunkenly: 'Charley, see that silly old woman over there? Calls himself General Commanding! Doesn't know where he is; doesn't know where his division is; can't even read a map properly. He's marched the poor devils off their feet and left his supplies behind, God knows how far back. They've had to use their iron rations and what they could pick up in the villages. And tomorrow he's going to fight a battle. Doesn't know anything about battles; the men have never been in trenches before, and tomorrow's going to be a glorious muck-up, and the day after tomorrow he'll be sent home.' Then he ended, quite seriously: 'Really, Charley, it's just like that, no exaggeration. You mark my words!'

That night we marched back again to Cambrin. Then we heard that the Middlesex would go over first, with us in support; and to their left the Second Argyll and Sutherland Highlanders, with the Cameronians in support. The young Royal Welch officers complained loudly at our not being given the honour of leading the attack. An hour or so past midnight we moved into trench sidings just in front of the village. Half a mile of communication trench separated us from the firing-line. At half past five the gas would be discharged. We were cold, tired, sick, and not at all in the mood for a battle, but tried to snatch an hour or two of sleep squatting in the trench. It had been raining for some time.

A grey, watery dawn broke at last behind the German lines; the bombardment, surprisingly slack all night, brisked up a little. 'Why the devil don't they send them over quicker?' complained an officer known as The Actor. 'This isn't my idea of a bombardment. We're getting nothing opposite us. What little there seems to be, is going into the Hohenzollern Redoubt.'

'Shell shortage. Expected it,' was Thomas's laconic reply.

We were told afterwards that on the 23rd a German aeroplane had bombed the Army Reserve shell-dump and sent it up. The bombardment on the 24th, and on the day of the battle itself, compared very poorly with that of the previous days. Thomas looked strained and ill. 'It's time they were sending that damned accessory off. I wonder what's doing.'

The events of the next few minutes are difficult for me now to sort out. I found it more difficult still at the time. All we heard back there in the sidings was a distant cheer, confused crackle of rifle-fire, yells, heavy shelling on our front line, more shouts and yells, and a continuous rattle of machine-guns. After a few minutes, lightly wounded men of the Middlesex came stumbling towards the dressing-station. I stood at the junction of the siding and the Alley which led to the dressing-station.

'What's happened? What's happened?' I asked.

'B—— muck-up,' was the most detailed answer I could get.

Among the wounded were a number of men yellow-faced and choking, their buttons tarnished green—gas cases. Then came the badly wounded. The route being narrow, the

82

stretchers had difficulty in getting down. The Germans started shelling it with five-point-nines.

Thomas went back to battalion headquarters through the shelling to ask for orders. It was the same place that I had visited on my first night in the trenches. This cluster of dug-outs in the reserve line showed very plainly from the air as battalion headquarters, and should never have been occupied during a battle. Just before Thomas arrived, the Germans put five shells into it. The adjutant jumped one way, the colonel another, the R.S.M. a third. One shell went into the signals dug-out, killed some signallers and destroyed the telephone. The colonel, slightly cut on the hand, joined the stream of wounded and was carried back as far as the base with it. The adjutant took command.

Meanwhile 'A' Company had been waiting in the siding. We fixed bayonets in readiness to go up and attack as soon as Captain Thomas returned with orders. Hundreds of wounded streamed by. At last Thomas's orderly appeared. 'Captain's orders, sir: "A" Company to move up to the front line.' The Actor gave the order 'Company forward!' The company advanced with a clatter of steel.

It seems that at half past four an R.E. captain commanding the gas-company in the front line phoned through to divisional headquarters: 'Dead calm. Impossible discharge accessory.' The answer he got was: 'Accessory to be discharged at all costs.' Thomas had not overestimated the gas-company's efficiency. The spanners for unscrewing the cocks of the cylinders proved, with two or three exceptions, to be misfits. The gas-men rushed about shouting for the loan of an adjust-able spanner. They managed to discharge one or two cylinders; the gas went whistling out, formed a thick cloud a few yards off in no-man's-land, and then gradually spread back into our trenches. The Germans, who had been expecting gas, im-mediately put on their gas-helmets: semi-rigid ones, better than ours. Bundles of oily cotton-waste were strewn along the

German parapet and set alight as a barrier to the gas. Then their batteries opened on our lines. The confusion in the front trench must have been horrible; direct hits broke several of the gas-cylinders, the trench filled with gas, the gas-company stampeded.

No orders could come through because the shell in the signals dug-out at battalion headquarters had cut communication not only between companies and battalion, but between battalion and division. The officers in the front trench had to decide on immediate action; so two companies of the Middlesex, instead of waiting for the intense bombardment which would follow the advertised forty minutes of gas, charged at once and got as far as the German wire—which our artillery had not yet cut. So far it had been treated only with shrapnel, which had no effect on it; the barbed-wire needed high-explosive, and plenty of it. The Germans shot the Middlesex men down. One platoon is said to have found a gap and got into the German trench. But there were no survivors of the platoon to confirm this. The Argyll and Sutherland Highlanders went over, also, on the Middlesex left; but two companies, instead of charging at once, rushed back out of the gas-filled assault trench to the support line, and attacked from there. They were held up by some old wire and were caught and machine-gunned by the Germans.

The survivors of the two leading Middlesex companies now lay in shell-craters close to the German wire, sniping and making the Germans keep their heads down. They had bombs to throw, but these were nearly all of a new type issued for the battle. The fuses were lighted on the match-box principle, and the rain had made them useless. The other two companies of the Middlesex soon followed in support. Machine-gun-fire stopped them half-way.

At this point the Royal Welch Fusiliers came up through heavy shell-fire. There was a continual scramble backwards and forwards, to cries of: 'Come on!' 'Get back!' 'Gas turning on us!' 'Keep your heads, you men!' 'Back like hell, boys!' 'Whose orders?' 'What's happening?' 'Gas!' 'Back!' 'Come on!' 'Gas!' 'Back!' Wounded men and stretcher-bearers kept trying to squeeze past. We were alternately putting on and taking off our gas-helmets, which made things worse. In many places the trench had caved in, obliging us to scramble over the top.

'B' Company reached the front line with only fifty men, the rest having lost their way in some abandoned trenches half-way up. The company commander blew his whistle and the company charged. They were stopped by machine-gun-fire before they had got through our own entanglements. The company commander died—oddly enough, of heart-failure—as he stood on the parapet.

A few minutes later, Captain Samson, with 'C' Company and the remainder of 'B', reached our front line. Finding the gas-cylinders still whistling and the trench full of dying men, he decided to go over too—he could not have it said that the Royal Welch had let down the Middlesex.

One of 'C' officers told me later what happened. It had been agreed to advance by platoon rushes with supporting fire. When his platoon had gone about twenty yards, he signalled them to lie down and open covering fire. The din was tremendous. He saw the platoon on his left flopping down too, so he whistled the advance again. Nobody seemed to hear. He jumped up from his shell-hole, waved and signalled 'Forward!'

Nobody stirred.

He shouted: 'You cowards, are you leaving me to go on alone?'

His platoon-sergeant, groaning with a broken shoulder, gasped: 'Not cowards, sir. Willing enough. But they're all blinking dead.' A machine-gun, traversing, had caught them as they rose to the whistle.

My own company, 'A' Company, had become separated by the shelling. I was with the leading platoon. Thomas brought up the remainder of the company and, with 'D', we waited for the whistle to follow the other two companies over. Fortunately at this moment the adjutant appeared. He was now left in command of the battalion, and told Thomas that he didn't care a damn about orders; he was going to cut his losses and not send 'A' and 'D' over to their deaths until he got definite orders from brigade. He had sent a runner back, and we must wait.

Meanwhile, the intense bombardment that was to follow the forty minutes' discharge of gas began. It concentrated on the German front trench and wire. A good many shells fell short, and we had further casualties from them. In no-man's-land, the survivors of the Middlesex and of our 'B' and 'C' Companies suffered heavily.

Rumours came down the trench of a disaster similar to our own in the brick-stack sector, where the Fifth Brigade had gone over; and again at Givenchy, where men of the Sixth Brigade at the Duck's Bill salient had fought their way into the enemy trenches, but been repulsed, their supply of bombs failing.

My memory of that day is hazy. We spent it getting the wounded down to the dressing-station, spraying the trenches and dug-outs to get rid of the gas, and clearing away the earth where trenches were blocked. Late in the afternoon we watched through our field-glasses the advance of reserves under heavy shell-fire towards Loos and Hill 70; it looked like a real breakthrough in that direction.

At dusk, we all went out to get in the wounded, leaving only sentries in the line. The Germans behaved generously. I do not remember hearing a shot fired that night, though we kept on until it was nearly dawn and we could see plainly; then they fired a few warning shots, and we gave it up. By this time we had recovered all the wounded, and most of the Royal Welch dead. The Argyll and Sutherland had seven hundred casualties, including fourteen officers killed out of

86

the sixteen who went over; the Middlesex, five hundred and fifty casualties, including eleven officers killed.

Three Middlesex officers, returning to the trenches with a few stragglers, reported at their headquarters. They were Choate, Henry and Hill. Hill told me the story of their reception. The colonel and the adjutant were sitting down to a meat pie when he and Henry arrived. Henry said: 'Come to report, sir. Ourselves and about ninety men of all companies. Mr Choate is back, unwounded, too.'

They looked up dully. 'So you've survived, have you?' the colonel said. 'Well, all the rest are dead. I suppose Mr Choate had better command what's left of "A" Company; the bombing officer will command what's left of "B" (the bombing officer had not gone over, but remained with headquarters); Mr Henry goes to "C" Company, Mr Hill to "D". The Royal Welch are holding the front line. We are here in support. Let me know where to find you if you're needed. Good night.'

Not having been offered a piece of meat pie or a drink of whisky, they saluted and went miserably out.

The adjutant called them back. 'Mr Hill! Mr Henry!'
'Sir?'

Hill said that he expected a change of mind as to the propriety with which hospitality could be offered by a regular colonel and adjutant to temporary second-lieutenants in distress. But it was only: 'Mr Hill, Mr Henry, I saw some men in the trench just now with their shoulder-straps unbuttoned and their equipment fastened anyhow. See that this does not occur in future. That's all.'

Henry heard the colonel from his bunk complaining that he had only two blankets and that it was a deucedly cold night.

Meanwhile, I took command of what remained of 'B' Company. Only six company officers survived in the Royal Welch. Next morning we were only five. Thomas was killed by a sniper while despondently watching through field-glasses the return of the New Army troops on the right. Pushed blindly into the gap made by the advance of the Seventh and Forty-seventh Divisions on the previous afternoon, they did not know where they were or what they were supposed to do. Their ration supply broke down, so they flocked back, not in panic, but stupidly, like a crowd returning from a cup final, with shrapnel bursting above them. We could scarcely believe our eyes, it was so odd.

The Actor took command of 'A' Company. We lumped 'A' and 'B' Companies together for the sake of relieving each other on night watch and getting some sleep. We had spent the day after the attack carrying the dead down for burial and cleaning the trench up as best we could. That night the Middlesex held the line, while the Royal Welch carried all the unbroken gas-cylinders along to a position on the left flank of the brigade, where they were to be used on the following night, September 27th. Only the officers knew of the proposed attack; the men must not be told until just beforehand. Rain was still pouring down, harder than ever. We knew definitely, this time, that ours would be only a diversion to help troops on our right make the real attack.

The scheme was the same as before: at 4 p.m. gas would be discharged for forty minutes, and after a quarter of an hour's bombardment we should attack. I broke the news to the men about three o'clock. They took it well.

At 4 p.m. then, the gas went off again with a strong wind; the gas-men had brought enough spanners this time. The Germans stayed absolutely silent. Flares went up from the reserve lines, and it looked as though all the men in the front trench were dead. The brigadier decided not to take too much for granted; after the bombardment he sent out a Cameronian officer and twenty-five men as a feeling-patrol. The patrol reached the German wire; there came a burst of machine-gun and rifle-fire, and only two wounded men regained the trench.

We waited on the fire-step from four to nine o'clock, with fixed bayonets, for the order to go over. At nine o'clock brigade called off the attack; we were told to hold ourselves in readiness to go over at dawn. No order came at dawn and no more attacks were promised us after this. From the morning of September 24th to the night of October 3rd, I had in all eight hours of sleep.

On the morning of the 27th a cry arose from no-man's-land. A wounded soldier of the Middlesex had recovered consciousness after two days. He lay close to the German wire. Our men heard it and looked at each other. We had a tender-hearted lance-corporal named Baxter. He was the man to boil up a special dixie for the sentries of his section when they came off duty. As soon as he heard the wounded Middlesex man, he ran along the trench calling for a volunteer to help fetch him in. Of course, no one would go; it was death to put one's head over the parapet. When he came running to ask me I excused myself as being the only officer in the company. I would come out with him at dusk, I said—not now. So he went alone. He jumped quickly over the parapet, then strolled across no-man's-land, waving a handkerchief; the Germans fired to frighten him, but since he persisted they let him come up close. Baxter continued towards them and, when he got to the Middlesex man, stopped and pointed to show the Germans what he was at. Then he dressed the man's wounds, gave him a drink of rum and some biscuit that he had with him, and promised to be back again at nightfall. He did come back, with a stretcher-party, and the man eventually recovered. I recommended Baxter for the Victoria Cross, being the only officer who had witnessed the action, but the authorities thought it worth no more than a Distinguished Conduct Medal.

On October 3rd we were relieved and went back to Annezin to recover and reorganize.

12

A T Annezin some of the lightly wounded rejoined for duty,
and a big draft from the Third Battalion arrived, so that
within a week we were nearly seven hundred strong, with a
full supply of officers. In the village I lodged with a withered
old woman called Adelphine Heu. She told me that all the girls
in Annezin prayed every night for the war to end, and for the
English to go away—as soon as their money was spent.

On the whole, troops serving in the Pas de Calais loathed
the French and found it difficult to sympathize with their mis-
fortunes. Also, we were shocked at the severity of French
national accountancy; when we were told, for instance, that
every British hospital train, the locomotive and carriages of
which had been imported from England, had to pay a £200
fee for use of the rails on each journey they made from railhead
to base.

Fighting still continued around Loos. We could hear the
guns in the distance, but the main thrust had clearly failed, and
we were now skirmishing for local advantages. Gradually the
noise died down, and at last a message came from brigade that
we would not be needed. So ended the operations for 1915.
Tension relaxed. We returned to battalion mess, to company
drill, and to riding-school for the young officers. There might
just as well have been no Battle of Loos, except that the senior

officers were fewer, and the Special Reserve element larger. On October 15th, I was gazetted a Special Reserve captain.

My remaining trench service with the Second Battalion that autumn proved uneventful; I found no excitement in patrolling, no horror in the continual experience of death. The single memorable event was one of purely technical interest: a new method that an officer named Owen and myself discovered for silencing machine-guns firing at night. We gave each sentry a piece of string about a yard long, with a cartridge tied at each end. When the machine-gun began traversing, sentries farthest from the line of fire would stretch their strings towards it and peg them down with cartridge points; so we got a pretty accurate line on the machine-gun. When we had about thirty or more of these lines taken on a single machine-gun, we fixed rifles as carefully as possible along them and waited; as soon as it started again we opened five rounds rapid. This gave a close concentration of fire, and no element of nervousness could disturb the aim, the rifles being secured between sandbags. The machine-gun stopped suddenly. Divisional headquarters asked us for a report of the method.

Having now been in the trenches for five months, I had passed my prime. For the first three weeks, an officer was of little use in the front line; he did not know his way about, had not learned the rules of health and safety, or grown accustomed to recognizing the degrees of danger. Between three weeks and four weeks he was at his best, unless he happened to have any particular bad shock or sequence of shocks. Then his usefulness gradually declined as neurasthenia developed. At six months he was still more or less all right; but by nine or ten months, unless he had been given a few weeks' rest on a technical course, or in hospital, he usually became a drag on the other company officers. After a year or fifteen months he was often worse than useless. Dr W. H. R. Rivers told me later that the action of one of the ductless glands—I think the adrenal— caused this slow general decline in military usefulness, by

o

pumping more and more of its sedative chemical into the bloodstream. With its continued assistance the man went about his tasks in an apathetic and doped condition, cheated into further endurance. It has taken some ten years for my blood to recover.

Officers had a less laborious but a more nervous time than the men. There were proportionately twice as many neurasthenic cases among officers as among men, though a man's average expectancy of trench service before getting killed or wounded was twice as long as an officer's. Officers between the ages of twenty-three and thirty-three could count on a longer useful life than those older or younger. I was too young. Men over forty, though not suffering from want of sleep so much as those under twenty, had less resistance to sudden alarms and shocks. The unfortunates were officers who had endured two years or more of continuous trench service. In many cases they became dipsomaniacs. I knew three or four who had worked up to the point of two bottles of whisky a day before being lucky enough to get wounded or sent home in some other way.

Apart from wounds, gas, and the accidents of war, the life of the trench soldier could not be called unhealthy while his ductless glands still functioned well. Plentiful food and hard work in the open air made up for the discomfort of wet feet, wet clothes and draughty billets. A continual need for alertness discouraged minor illnesses: a cold vanished in a few hours, an attack of indigestion passed almost unnoticed. This was true, at least, in a good battalion, where the men were bent on going home either with an honourable wound or not at all. In an inferior battalion, the men would prefer a wound to bronchitis, but not mind the bronchitis.

'Trench feet' seemed to be almost entirely a matter of morale, in spite of the lecture formula that N.C.O.s and officers used to repeat time after time to the men. It was caused by going to sleep with wet boots, cold feet, and depression. Wet

92

boots, by themselves, did not matter. If a man warmed his feet at a brazier, or stamped until they were warm, and then went off to sleep with a sandbag tied around them, he took no harm. He might even fall asleep with cold, wet feet, and find that they had swelled slightly owing to the pressure of his boots or puttees; but trench feet came only if he did not mind getting trench feet, or anything else—because his battalion had lost the power of sticking things out. At Bouchavesnes, on the Somme, in the winter of 1916–17, a battalion of dismounted cavalry lost half its strength in two days from trench feet; our Second Battalion had just completed ten days in the same trenches with no cases at all.

In November, much to my delight, I had orders to join the First Battalion, now reorganizing after the Loos fighting. I found it in billets at Locon, only a mile or so north of Cambrin. The difference between the two battalions continued markedly throughout the war. The difference was that, in August 1914, the Second Battalion had just finished its eighteen years' overseas tour, whereas the First Battalion had not left England since the South African War and was, therefore, less old-fashioned in its militarism and more humane. It would have been impossible there to see what I once saw in the Second—a senior officer pursuing a private soldier down the street, kicking his bottom because he had given a slack salute. The First Battalion was as efficient and regimental, on the whole even more successful in its fighting, and a much easier battalion to live in.

When I left the Second Battalion, the adjutant let me take my admirable servant, Private Fahy (known as 'Tottie Fay', after the actress), with me. Tottie, a reservist from Birmingham, had been called up when war broke out, and fought with the Second Battalion ever since. By trade a silversmith, he had recently gone on leave, and brought me back a gift cigarette case, all his own work, engraved with my name. On arrival at the First Battalion, however, he met one Sergeant Dickens.

They had been boozing chums in India seven or eight years ago, and joyfully celebrated the reunion. The next morning I was surprised and annoyed to find my buttons unpolished and only cold water for shaving; it made me late for breakfast. I could get no news of Tottie, but on my way to rifle inspection at nine o'clock at the company billet, noticed Field Punishment No. 1 being carried out in a corner of the farmyard. Tottie had been awarded twenty-eight days of it for 'drunkenness in the field', and stood spread-eagled to the wheel of a company limber, tied by the ankles and wrists in the form of an X. He was obliged to stay in this position—'Crucifixion' they called it—for several hours every day so long as the battalion remained in billets, and then again after the next spell of trenches. I shall never forget the look that my quiet, respectful, devoted Tottie gave me. He wanted to tell me that he regretted having let me down, and his immediate reaction was an attempt to salute. I could see him vainly trying to lift his hand to his forehead, and bring his heels together. The battalion police-sergeant, a fierce-looking man, had just finished knotting him up when I arrived. I told Tottie, for what that might be worth, that I was sorry to see him in trouble.

Sergeant Dickens was a different case: a born fighter, and one of the best N.C.O.s in either battalion of the regiment. He had won the Distinguished Conduct Medal and Bar, the Military Medal and the French Médaille Militaire; been two or three times promoted to sergeant's rank, and each time reduced for drunkenness. He always escaped the Field Punishment awarded for this crime, because it was considered sufficient disgrace if he merely lost his stripes; and as soon as a battle started would distinguish himself so conspicuously by his leadership that he would be given them back again.

Early in December we went for divisional training in the distant countryside. We stayed at a village called Montagne le Fayel for six weeks. Colonel Ford, known in the regiment as

'Scatter' (short for 'Scatter-cash' because, when he first joined, he had spent his allowance so lavishly), put the battalion through its paces with peacetime severity. The guns could only just be heard in the distance, and every man in the battalion was fit.

One day all officers and warrant-officers were hurriedly summoned to the village schoolroom. Scatter entered and glared at us from the teacher's desk. He began his lecture with general accusations, saying that he had lately noticed many signs of slovenliness in the battalion. He threatened to stop all leave to the United Kingdom unless matters improved, and promised us a saluting parade every morning before breakfast which he would attend in person. Then he continued: 'I have here principally to tell you of a very disagreeable occurrence. As I left my Orderly Room this morning, I came upon a group of soldiers; I will not particularize their company. One of these soldiers was in conversation with a lance-corporal. You may not believe me, but it is a fact that he addressed the corporal by his Christian name: *he called him Jack!* And the corporal made no protest! To think that the First Battalion has sunk to a level where it is possible for such familiarity to exist between N.C.O.s and the men under their command! Naturally, I put the corporal under arrest, and he appeared before me at once on the charge of 'conduct unbecoming to an N.C.O.'. I reduced him to the ranks, and awarded the man Field Punishment for using insubordinate language to an N.C.O. But I warn you, if any further case of this sort comes to my notice—and I expect you officers to report the slightest instance to me at once—instead of dealing with it as a company matter . . .'

This is one of those caricature scenes that now seems to sum up the various stages of my life. Myself in faultless khaki with highly polished buttons and belt, revolver at hip, whistle on cord, delicate moustache on upper lip, and stern endeavour a-glint in either eye, pretending to be a Regular Army captain;

but crushed into an inky desk like an overgrown schoolboy. A fresco ran around the walls of the classroom illustrating the evils of alcoholism. It started with the innocent boy being offered a drink by his mate, and then showed his downward path of degradation, culminating in wife-beating, murder, and *delirium tremens*; but, at least, he never went so far as to call his lance-corporal 'Jack'!

At New Year, the Seventh Division sent two company officers from each brigade to instruct troops at the base. I and a Queen's captain happened to be the two who had been out longest, so we were given this gift of eight weeks' additional life. At the Harfleur 'Bull Ring' newly-arrived drafts went for technical instruction before going up the line. I taught troops trench relief and trench discipline in a model system of trenches. My principal other business was arms-drill.

In March I rejoined the First Battalion on the Somme. It was the primrose season. We went in and out of the Fricourt trenches, with billets at Morlancourt, a country village still untouched by shell-fire. (Later it got knocked to pieces; the Australians and the Germans captured and recaptured it from each other several times, until only the site remained.)

Our greatest trial was the German canister—a two-gallon drum with a cylinder inside containing about two pounds of an explosive called ammonal that looked like salmon paste, smelled like marzipan and, when it went off, sounded like the Day of Judgement. The hollow around the cylinder contained scrap metal, apparently collected by French villagers behind the German lines: rusty nails, fragments of British and French shells, spent bullets, and the screws, nuts and bolts that heavy lorries leave behind on the road. We dissected one unexploded canister, and found in it, among other things, the cog-wheels of a clock and half a set of false teeth. The canister could easily be heard approaching and looked harmless in the air, but its shock was as shattering as the very heaviest shell. It would blow in any but the very deepest dug-outs; and the false

96

teeth, rusty nails, cog-wheels and so on went flying all over the place. We could not agree how the Germans fired a weapon of that size. The problem remained unsolved until July 1st, when the battalion attacked from these same trenches and discovered a wooden cannon buried in the earth and discharged with a time-fuse. The crew offered to surrender, but our men had sworn for months to get them.

We were issued with a new gas-helmet. It differed from the previous models. One breathed in through the nose from inside the helmet, and breathed out through a special valve held in the mouth; but I could not manage this. Boxing with an already broken nose had recently displaced the septum, which forced me to breathe through my mouth. In a gas-attack, I would be unable to use the helmet—the only type claimed to be proof against the newest German gas. The battalion doctor advised a nose-operation as soon as possible.

I took his advice, and missed being with the First Battalion when the expected offensive started. Three out of five of my fellow-officers were killed in it.

13

I WENT on leave in April 1916. At the first opportunity I went to the Milbank Military Hospital in London, where I had my nose operated on free by an Army surgeon. In peacetime this would have cost me sixty guineas, and another twenty guineas in nursing-home fees. On the other hand, I should have been able to pick my specialist; this one bungled the job, and I still cannot breathe properly through one nostril.

When my leave expired I rejoined the Third Battalion at Litherland, near Liverpool, where it had been shifted from Wrexham as part of the Mersey defence force. I remember that one night in the mess an old major laid it down axiomatically that every so-called sportsman had at some time or other committed a sin against sportsmanship. When challenged to make good this slander, he cross-examined each of his neighbours in turn, putting them on their honour to tell the truth.

One of them, blushing, admitted that he had once shot grouse two days before the Twelfth: 'I was sailing next day to rejoin the battalion in India and this was my last chance.' Another said that when a public-school boy, and old enough to know better, he had killed a sitting pheasant with a stone. Another had gone out with a poacher—in his Sandhurst days—and crumbled poison-berry into a trout-stream. An even more scandalous confession came from a New Army major, a gentleman-farmer: that his estate had been overrun by foxes one year and, the headquarters of the nearest hunt being thirty miles away, he had permitted his bailiff to protect the hen roosts with a gun. Then came the turn of the medical officer, who said: 'Well, once while I was a student at St Andrews, a friend asked me to put ten bob for him on a horse in the Lincolnshire. I couldn't find my bookmaker in time. The horse lost, but I never returned the ten bob.' At this, one of the guests, an officer in the King's Own Scottish Borderers, suddenly grew excited, jumped up and leaned over the table, doubling his fists. 'And was not the name of the horse Strathspey? And will you not pay me my ten shillings now immediately?'

I stayed at Litherland a few weeks only. On July 1st, 1916, the Somme offensive began, and all available trained men and officers went out to replace casualties. I had the pleasure of riding up the line on a locomotive and helping the French stoker, thus fulfilling a childhood dream; though bitterly disappointed at finding myself posted to the Second Battalion, not the First.

The Second Battalion was in trenches at Givenchy, on the other side of the canal from the Cuinchy brick-stacks. I arrived on July 5th, to find one of our raids in progress. Prisoners were already coming down the trench, scared and chattering to each other: Saxons, just back from a divisional rest and a week's leave to Germany, with new uniforms and their packs full of good lootable stuff.

It was a retaliatory raid. Only a few days before, the Germans had sent up the biggest mine blown on the Western front so far. It caught our 'B' Company. The crater must have been about thirty yards across. There were few survivors of 'B' Company. The Germans had then come over in force to catch the other companies in confusion. Stanway, who had been a company sergeant-major during the retreat, and was now a major, rallied some men on the flank and drove the Germans back.

This raid had been Stanway's revenge. He and Colonel 'Tibs' Crawshay—the depôt adjutant who had originally sent me out to France—planned it most elaborately, with bombardments and smoke-screen diversion on the flanks. A barrage of shrapnel would shift forward and back from the German front line to the supports. The intention was that the Germans should go down into the shell-proof dug-outs at the first bombardment, leaving only sentries in the trench, and reappear as soon as the barrage lifted. When it started again, they would make another dash for the dug-outs. After this had happened two or three times they would be slow in emerging. Then, under cover of a smoke-screen, the raid would be made and the barrage put down uninterruptedly on the support and reserve lines, to prevent reinforcements from coming up.

My only part in the raid, which proved very successful, was to make a detailed report of it at Crawshay's request—not the report for divisional headquarters, but a page of history to be sent to the depôt for filing in regimental records. I noted that for the first time since the eighteenth century the regiment had reverted to the pike: instead of rifle and bayonet, some of the raiders had used butchers' knives secured with medical plaster to the ends of broomsticks. This pike, a lighter weapon than rifle and bayonet, was a useful addition to bombs and revolvers.

Four days after the raid we marched through Béthune, now much knocked about and nearly deserted, and there entrained for the Somme. On July 14th we came to the original front line. The fighting had moved two miles on. At 4 a.m. on July 15th, we reached the more recent battle area. Wounded and prisoners came streaming past in the half-light. We marched by platoons, at fifty yards' distance. Just beyond Fricourt a German shell-barrage made the road impassable, so we left it and moved forward over thickly shell-pitted ground until 8 a.m., when we found ourselves on the fringe of Mametz Wood, among the dead of our own New Army battalions who had helped to capture it. There we halted in thick mist. The Germans had been using lachrymatory shell, and the mist held the fumes, making us cough.

When the mist cleared, we learnt that the battalion's next objective was 'The Quadrangle', a small copse where Siegfried Sassoon distinguished himself by taking, single-handed, a battalion frontage which the Royal Irish Regiment had failed to take the day before. He went over with bombs in daylight, under covering fire from a couple of rifles, and scared away the occupants. A pointless feat, since instead of signalling for reinforcements, he sat down in the German trench and began reading a book of poems which he had brought with him. When he finally went back he did not even report. Colonel Stockwell, then in command, raged at him. The attack on Mametz Wood had been delayed for two hours because British patrols were still reported to be out. 'British patrols' were Siegfried and his book of poems. 'I'd have got you a D.S.O., if you'd only shown more sense,' stormed Stockwell. Siegfried had been doing heroic things ever since I left the battalion. His nickname in the Seventh Division was 'Mad Jack'. He won a Military Cross for bringing in a wounded lance-corporal from a mine-crater close to the German lines, under heavy fire.

I had been posted to 'D' Company. On the way up through the ruins, we were shelled with gas-shells. The standing order with regard to gas-shells was not to bother about respirators, but push on. Hitherto, they had all been lachrymatory ones; these were the first of the deadly kind, so we lost half a dozen men.

When at last 'D' Company reached the trenches, scooped beside a road and not more than three feet deep, the badly shaken Tyneside company we were relieving hurried off, without any of the usual formalities. I asked one of their officers where the Germans were. He said he didn't know, but pointed vaguely towards a place a mile to our front. Then I asked him who held our left flank, and how far off they were. He didn't know. I damned his soul to Hell as he went away. Having got into touch with 'C' Company behind us on the right, and the Fourth Suffolks fifty yards to the left, we began deepening the trenches and presently located the Germans— in a trench-system five hundred yards to our front, keeping fairly quiet.

The next day, at dinner-time, very heavy shelling started: shells bracketed along the trench about five yards short and five yards over, but never quite got it. That afternoon the company got an order from brigade to build two cruciform strong-points at such-and-such a map reference. Moodie, the company commander, and I looked at our map and laughed. Moodie sent back a message that he would be glad to obey, but would first need an artillery bombardment and considerable reinforcements, because the points selected, half-way to Martinpuich, were occupied by the enemy. Colonel Crawshay came up and verified this. He told us to build the strong-points about three hundred yards forward and two hundred yards apart. So one platoon stayed behind in the trench, and the others went out and began digging. A cruciform strong-point consisted of two trenches, each some thirty yards long, crossing at right angles in the middle; being wired all round, it looked, in diagram, like a hot-cross bun. The defenders could bring fire to bear against attack from any direction. We were to hold these points with a Lewis gun and a platoon of men apiece.

The next evening, July 19th, we were relieved and told that we would be attacking High Wood, which could be seen a thousand yards away to the right at the top of a slope. Two British brigades had already attempted it; in both cases a counter-attack drove them out again. The Royal Welch were now reduced by casualties to about four hundred strong, including transport, stretcher-bearers, cooks and other non-combatants. I took command of 'B' Company.

We lay on the reverse slope of a slight ridge, about half a mile from the wood. I attended the meeting of company commanders; Colonel Crawshay told us the plan. 'Look here, you fellows,' he said, 'we're in reserve for this attack. The Cameronians and the Fifth Scottish Rifles are going up to the wood first; that's at 5 a.m. The Public Schools Battalion are in support should anything go wrong. I don't know whether we shall be called on; if we are, it will mean that the Jocks have legged it. The Public Schools Battalion is, well, what we know it is; so if we're called for, that will be the end of us.' He said this with a laugh, and we all laughed.

We were sitting on the ground, protected by a road-bank; a battery of French 75's began firing rapid over our heads from about twenty yards away. There was an even greater concentration of guns in Happy Valley now. We could hardly hear the colonel's words. He said goodbye and good luck, and we rejoined our companies.

At this juncture the usual inappropriate message came through from division. Division could always be trusted to send a warning about verdigris on vermorel-sprayers, or the keeping of pets in trenches, or being polite to our allies, or some other triviality, exactly when an attack was in progress. This time orders came for a private in 'C' Company to report immediately, under escort of a lance-corporal, to the assistant provost-marshal back at Albert, where a court-martial had been convened. A sergeant of the company must also report as a witness in the case. The private was charged with the murder of a French civilian in an *estaminet* at Béthune a month previously. It seems that a good deal of cognac had been going round, and the French civilian, who bore a grudge against the British because of his faithless wife, began to insult the private. He was reported, somewhat improbably, as having said: '*Anglais no bon, Allmand très bon. War fineesh, napoo les Anglais. Allmand win.*' The private had thereupon drawn his bayonet and run the man through. At the court-martial the private was exonerated; the French civil representative commending him for having 'energetically repressed local defeatism'. So he and two N.C.O.s missed the battle.

What sort of a battle they missed I pieced together afterwards. The Jocks did get into the wood, and the Royal Welch were not called on to reinforce until eleven o'clock in the morning. The Germans put down a barrage along our ridge where we were lying, and we lost a third of the battalion before the show started. I was one of the casualties.

The German batteries were handing out heavy stuff and so much of it that we decided to move back fifty yards at a rush. As we did so, an eight-inch shell burst three paces behind me. I heard the explosion, and felt as though I had been punched rather hard between the shoulder-blades, but without any pain. I took the punch merely for the shock of the explosion; but blood trickled into my eye and, turning faint, I called to Moodie: 'I've been hit.' Then I fell. A minute or two before I had got two very small wounds on my left hand; and in exactly the same position as the two that drew blood from my right hand during the preliminary bombardment at Loos.

One piece of shell went through my left thigh, high up, near the groin. The wound over the eye was made by a little chip of marble, possibly from one of the cemetery headstones. This, and a finger-wound which split the bone, probably came from another shell bursting in front of me. But a piece of shell had also gone in two inches below the point of my right shoulder-blade and came out through my chest two inches above the right nipple.

My memory of what happened then is vague. Apparently Dr Dunn came up through the barrage with a stretcher-party, dressed my wound, and got me down to a dressing-station. I remember being put on the stretcher, and winking at the stretcher-bearer sergeant who had just said: 'Old Gravy's got it, all right!' They laid my stretcher in a corner of the dressing-station, where I remained unconscious for more than twenty-four hours.

Late that night, Colonel Crawshay came back from High Wood and visited the dressing-station; he saw me lying in the corner, and they told him I was done for. The next morning, July 21st, clearing away the dead, they found me still breathing and put me on an ambulance for Heilly, the nearest field hospital. The pain of being jolted down the Happy Valley, with a shell-hole at every three or four yards of the road, woke me up. I remember screaming. But back on the better roads I became unconscious again. That morning, Crawshay wrote the usual formal letters of condolence to the next-of-kin of the six of seven officers who had been killed. This was his letter to my mother.

22.7.16

Dear Mrs Graves,

I very much regret to have to write and tell you your son has died of wounds. He was very gallant, and was doing so well and is a great loss.

He was hit by a shell and very badly wounded, and died on the way down to the base I believe. He was not in bad pain, and our doctor managed to get across and attend to him at once.

We have had a very hard time, and our casualties have been large. Believe me you have all our sympathy in your loss, and we have lost a very gallant soldier.

Please write to me if I can tell you or do anything.

Yours sincerely,
C. Crawshay, Lt.-Col.

Then he made out the official casualty list—a long one, because only eighty men were left in the battalion—and reported me 'died of wounds'. Heilly lay on the railway; close to the station stood the hospital tents with the red cross prominently painted on the roofs, to discourage air-bombing. Fine July weather made the tents insufferably hot. I was semi-conscious now, and aware of my lung-wound through a shortness of breath.

The nights of the 22nd and 23rd were horrible. Early on the morning of the 24th, when the doctor came round the ward, I said: 'You must send me away from here. This heat will kill me.' It was beating on my head through the canvas.

'Stick it out. Your best chance is to lie here and not to be moved. You'd not reach the base alive.'

'Let me risk the move. I'll be all right, you'll see.'

Half an hour later he returned. 'Well, you're having it your way. I've just got orders to evacuate every case in the hospital. Apparently the Guards have been in it up at Delville Wood, and they'll all be coming down tonight.' I did not fear that I would die, now—it was enough to be honourably wounded and bound for home.

Later, I managed to find out what had happened at High Wood. Captain Colbart of the Fifth Scottish Rifles has recently written to me:

> We attacked on the right, the Cameronians on the left, taking our objectives and sundry Germans. After midday I was the only officer left in our battalion. At about 9 a.m., the troops on the left fell back before a counter-attack— they didn't try to fight, as far as I saw. They were all mixed up—Cameronians, Scottish Rifles, Public Schools Battalion. The débâcle was stopped in mid-wood, and my company on the right retook our objective. I was holding a strong-point at the east corner of the wood, which we had built according to orders, when the Royal Welch came up under Moodie. They attacked north-west and took the whole wood. Colonel Crawshay had his headquarters at

the south corner; I reported to him there, and then rejoined my troops when the Germans counter-attacked with heavy artillery support at about 5 p.m. under heavy shell-fire.

Crawshay reported to brigade that he had captured the wood but would not be responsible for holding it unless reinforcements came up at once. By the time these arrived, the Germans had got a footing in the north-west corner. We were relieved by the Ninety-eighth Brigade of our own Division.

That evening, the R.A.M.C. orderlies dared not lift me from the stretcher into a hospital train bunk, for fear of starting haemorrhage in the lung. So they laid the stretcher above it, with the handles resting on the head-rail and foot-rail. I had then been on the same stretcher for five days. I remember the journey as a nightmare. My back was sagging, and I could not raise my knees to relieve the cramp, the bunk above me being only a few inches away. An orderly gave me a pencil and paper, and I wrote home to my mother: 'I am wounded, but all right.' This was July 24th, my twenty-first birthday, and also the official date of my death. She got the letter two days after that written by the colonel. At home they could not decide whether my letter had been written just before I died and misdated, or whether I had died just after writing it. 'Died of wounds', however, seemed so much more circumstantial than 'killed' that, on receipt of a long telegram from the Army Council confirming my death, they gave me up. I found myself in No. 8 Hospital at Rouen—an ex-château high above the town. The next day my Aunt Susan came from the South of France to visit a South Wales Borderer nephew in the same hospital, whose leg had just been amputated. Happening to see my name listed on the door of the ward, she gave me some of the nectarines intended for him, and wrote to reassure my mother. On the 30th, Colonel Crawshay sent me a letter:

Dear von Runicke,*

I cannot tell you how pleased I am you are alive. I was told your number was up for certain, and a letter was supposed to have come in from Field Ambulance saying you had gone under.

Well, it's good work. We had a rotten time, and after succeeding in doing practically the impossible we collected that rotten crowd and put them in their places, but directly dark came they legged it. It was too sad.

We lost heavily. It is not fair putting brave men like ours alongside that crowd. I also wish to thank you for your good work and bravery, and only wish you could have been with them. I have read of bravery but I have never seen such magnificent and wonderful disregard for death as I saw that day. It was almost uncanny—it was so great. I once heard an old officer in the Royal Welch say the men would follow you to Hell; but these chaps would bring you back and put you in a dug-out in Heaven.

Good luck and a quick recovery. I shall drink your health tonight.

'Tibs.'

I had much discomfort from the shortness of my breath; I contrasted the pain and discomfort favourably with that of the operation on my nose two months previously; for which I had won no sympathy at all, because it was not a war injury.

A day or two later I sailed back to England by hospital ship.

* My regimental nickname.

14

FROM Waterloo Station an ambulance took me to Queen Alexandra's Hospital at Highgate, reputedly the best hospital in London. There the lung healed up easily, and the doctors saved my finger. I heard there for the first time of my supposed death. The joke contributed greatly to my recovery. People with whom I had been on the worst terms during my life, wrote the most enthusiastic condolences to my mother. I have kept a letter from *The Times* advertising manager, dated August 5th, 1916:

Captain Robert Graves.

Dear Sir,

We have to acknowledge receipt of your letter with reference to the announcement contradicting the report of your death from wounds. Having regard, however, to the fact that we had previously published some biographical details, we inserted your announcement in our issue of today (Saturday) under 'Court Circular' without charge, and we have much pleasure in enclosing herewith cutting of same.

Yours, etc.

The cutting read:

> Captain Robert Graves, Royal Welch Fusiliers, officially reported died of wounds, wishes to inform his friends that he is recovering from his wounds at Queen Alexandra's Hospital, Highgate, N.

The only inconvenience caused by this death was that Cox's Bank stopped my pay, and I had difficulty in persuading it to honour my cheques. Siegfried Sassoon wrote of his joy at hearing I was alive again. He had been sent back to England with suspected lung trouble and felt nine parts dead from the horror of the Somme fighting. We agreed to take our leave together at Harlech when I got well enough to travel. I was able to travel in September. We met on Paddington Station. Siegfried bought a copy of *The Times* at the bookstall. As usual, we turned to the casualty list first, and found there the names of practically every officer in the First Battalion, listed as either killed or wounded. It had happened at Ale Alley near Ginchy, on September 3rd. A dud show, with the battalion outflanked by a counter-attack.

In November, Siegfried and I rejoined the battalion at Litherland, and shared a hut. We decided not to make any public protest against war. Siegfried said that we must 'keep up the good reputation of the poets'—as men of courage, he meant. Our best place would be back in France, away from the more shameless madness of home-service. There, our function would not be to kill Germans, though that might happen, but to make things easier for the men under our command. For them, the difference between being commanded by someone whom they could count as a friend—someone who protected them as much as he could from the grosser indignities of the military system—and having to study the whims of any petty tyrant in an officer's tunic, made all the difference in the world.

In December, I attended a medical board; they sounded my chest and asked how I was feeling. The president wanted to know whether I wanted a few months more home-service. I said: 'No, sir, I should be much obliged if you would pass me fit for service overseas.' In January I got my sailing orders.

I went back an old soldier, as my kit and baggage proved. I had reduced the original Christmas-tree to a pocket-torch with a fourteen-day battery, and a pair of insulated wire-cutters strong enough to cut German wire (the ordinary Army issue would cut only British wire). Instead of a haversack, I bought a pack like the ones carried by the men, but lighter and waterproof. I had lost my revolver when wounded and not bought another; a rifle and bayonet could always be got from the battalion. (Not carrying rifle and bayonet made officers conspicious during an attack; in most divisions now they carried them; and also wore trousers rolled down over their puttees, like the men, instead of riding-breeches—because the Germans had learned to recognize officers by their 'thin knees'.)

I commanded a draft of ten young officers. Young officers, at this period, were expected, as someone has noted in his war memoirs, to be roistering blades over wine and women. These ten did their best. Three of them got venereal disease at Rouen.

I found the Second Battalion near Bouchavesnes on the Somme, but a very different Second Battalion. No riding-school, no battalion mess, no regular officers, except for a couple of newly arrived Sandhurst boys. I was more warmly welcomed this time. But the day before I reported, Colonel Crawshay had been wounded while out in no-man's-land inspecting the battalion wire: shot in the thigh by one of the 'rotten crowd' of his letter, who mistook him for a German and fired without challenging. He has been in and out of nursing homes ever since.

Dr Dunn asked me with kindly disapproval, what I meant

by returning so soon. I said: 'I couldn't stand England any longer.' He told the acting C.O. that I was, in his opinion, unfit for trench service, so I took command of the headquarters company and went to live with the transport, back at Frises, where the Somme made a bend. My company consisted of regimental clerks, cooks, tailors, shoemakers, pioneers, transport men, and so on, who in a breakthrough could turn riflemen and be used as a combatant force, as at the First Battle of Ypres. We lived in dug-outs, close to the river, which was frozen over completely but for a narrow stretch of fast-running water in the middle. I have never been so cold in all my life. I used to go up to the trenches every night with the rations; it was about a twelve-mile walk there and back.

General Pinney, now commanding the Thirty-third Division, felt teetotal convictions on behalf of his men and stopped their issue of rum, unless in emergencies; the immediate result being the heaviest sick-list that the battalion had ever known. Our men looked forward to their tot of rum at the dawn stand-to as the brightest moment of the twenty-four hours; when this was denied them, their resistance weakened.

Our reserve billets for the Bouchavesnes trenches were at Suzanne: not really billets, but dug-outs and shelters. Suzanne also lay in ruins. This winter was the hardest since 1894–5. The men played inter-company football matches on the river, now frozen two feet thick. I remember a meal here, in a shelter-billet: stew and tinned tomatoes on aluminium plates. Though the food arrived hot from the kitchen next-door, ice had formed on the edge of our plates before we finished eating. In all this area one saw no French civilians, no un-shelled houses, no signs of cultivation. I have kept no records of this time, but the memory of its misery survives.

Brigade appointed me a member of a field general court-martial that was to sit on an Irish sergeant charged with 'shamefully casting away his arms in the presence of the enemy'. I had heard about the case unofficially; the man, maddened by an intense bombardment, had thrown away his rifle and run with the rest of his platoon. An army order, secret and confidential, addressed to officers of captain's rank and above, laid down that, in the case of men tried for their life on other charges, sentence might be mitigated if conduct in the field had been exemplary; but cowardice was punishable only with death, and no medical excuses could be accepted. Therefore I saw no choice between sentencing the man to death and refusing to take part in the proceedings. If I refused, I should be court-martialled myself, and a reconstituted court would sentence the sergeant to death anyhow. Yet I could not sign a death-verdict for an offence which I might have committed myself in similar circumstances. I evaded the dilemma. One other officer in the battalion, besides the acting C.O., had the necessary year's service as a captain entitling him to sit on a field general court-martial. I found him willing enough to take my place. He was hard-boiled and glad of a trip to Amiens, and I took over his duties.

Executions were frequent in France. I had my first direct experience of official lying when I arrived at Le Havre in May 1915, and read the back-files of army orders at the rest camp. They contained something like twenty reports of men shot for cowardice or desertion; yet a few days later the responsible minister in the House of Commons, answering a question from a pacifist, denied that sentence of death for a military offence had been carried out in France on any member of His Majesty's Forces.

A day or two later, because the acting C.O. was still sick, I found myself in temporary command of the battalion, and attended a commanding officers' conference at brigade headquarters. Opposite our trenches a German salient protruded, and the brigadier wanted to 'bite it off' in proof of the division's offensive spirit. Trench soldiers could never understand the Staff's desire to bite off an enemy salient. It was hardly desirable to be fired at from both flanks; if the Germans had got caught in a salient, our obvious duty must be to keep them there as long as they could be persuaded to stay. We concluded that a passion for straight lines, for which head-quarters were well known, had dictated this plan, which had no strategic or tactical excuse. The attack had been twice postponed, and twice cancelled.

Even a promise of special rum could not hearten the battalion. Everyone agreed that the attack was unnecessary, foolish, and impossible. A thaw had now set in, and the four company commanders assured me that to cross three hundred yards of no-man's-land, which constant shelling and the thaw had turned into a morass of mud more than knee-deep, would take even lightly armed troops four or five minutes. Not a man would be able to reach the enemy lines so long as a single section of Germans with rifles remained to defend them.

The general, when I arrived, inquired in a fatherly way whether I was not proud to be attending a commanding officers' conference at the age of twenty-one. I answered irritably that I had not examined my feelings, but that I was old enough soldier to realize the impossibility of the attack. The colonel of the Cameronians, who were also to be en-gaged, took the same line. So the brigadier finally called off the show. That night, I went up with rations as usual; the officers were much relieved to hear of my stand at the conference.

We had been heavily shelled on the way, and while I took a drink at battalion headquarters, someone sent me a message about a direct hit on 'D' Company limber. I found the shattered limber, and remains of the petrol tins, full of water, which it was carrying, but no sign of the team. They were highly valued horses, having won a prize at a divisional horse show some months previously. So Meredith the transport sergeant and I sent the transport back, and went looking for the horses in the dark. We stumbled through miles of morass that night, but could not find hoof or hide of them. We used to boast that our transport animals were the best in France, and our transport men the best horse-thieves. We had never lost a horse to any other battalion; so, naturally, Sergeant Meredith and I, who had started out with the rations at four o'clock in the afternoon, continued our search until long after midnight. When we reached Frises at 3 a.m. I collapsed on my bunk, completely exhausted.

The next day, Dr Dunn diagnosed bronchitis, and I went back in an ambulance to Rouen, once more to No. 8 Red Cross Hospital. The R.A.M.C. major recognized me and said: 'What on earth are *you* doing out in France, young man? If I find you and those lungs of yours in my hospital again, I'll have you court-martialled.'

Later I had a letter to say that the horses had been found shortly after I left—unhurt except for grazes on their bellies, and in possession of the Fourth Division machine-gun company. The machine-gunners were caught disguising them with stain, and trying to remove the regimental marks.

At Rouen they asked me where in England I should like to be hospitalized. I said, at random: 'Oxford.'

15

So I was sent to Oxford: to Somerville College which, like the Examination Schools, had been converted into a hospital. Deciding to stay in Oxford, I applied for an instructional job in one of the Officer–Cadet Battalions quartered in the men's colleges. They posted me to the Wadham Company of No. 4 Battalion. These battalions had grown out of instructional schools for young officers. The cadet course was three months—later increased to four—but a severe one. We taught drill and musketry, and 'conduct befitting officers and gentlemen', but chiefly tactical exercises with limited objectives.

Though the quality of the officers had deteriorated from the regimental point of view, their greater efficiency in action amply compensated for their deficiency in manners. The cadet-battalion system saved the Army in France from becoming a mere rabble. We failed about a sixth of the candidates for commissions; the failures were sometimes public-school boys without the necessary toughness, but usually men from France, recommended on compassionate grounds—rather stupid platoon-sergeants and machine-gun corporals who had been out too long and needed a rest. Our final selection was made by watching the candidates play games, principally rugger and soccer. Those who played rough but not dirty, and had quick reactions, were the sort needed, and we spent most of our spare time playing games with them. My platoon consisted of New Zealanders, Canadians, South Africans, two men from the Fiji Island contingent, an English farm labourer, a Welsh miner, and two or three public-school boys. Most of them were killed during the next year and a half of war.

The social system at Oxford had been dislocated. Mr J. V. Powell, the St John's don destined to be my moral tutor when I came up, now wore the grey uniform of a corporal in the General Reserve, drilled in the parks, and saluted me whenever we met. A college servant held a commission, and was instructing in the other cadet-battalion. There cannot have been more than a hundred and fifty undergraduates in residence at this time: American Rhodes Scholars, Indians, and the unfit.

The War Office then stopped the privilege that officers enjoyed, after leaving hospital, of going to their own homes for convalescence. It had been noticed that many of them took no trouble to get well and return to duty; they kept late nights, drank, and overtaxed their strength. Therefore, when somewhat recovered, I was sent to a convalescent home in the Isle of Wight—none other than Osborne Palace; my bedroom had once been the royal night-nursery of King Edward VII and his brothers and sisters. After staying here a little while I had to go and save a friend at Litherland from a court-martial so I applied to appear before a medical board that sat the next day, and asked the doctors to pass me fit for home service. I was not fit, and they knew it, but I asked it as a favour.

I returned to Litherland and achieved my object, but found that the president of the Osborne medical board had been right: I should not have been back on duty. The training at the camp was intensive, and being given command of a trained-men company I did not get enough rest. I realized how bad my nerves were when one day, marching through the streets of Litherland on a battalion route-march, I saw three workmen in gas-masks beside an open man-hole, bending over a corpse which they had just hauled up from a sewer. His clothes were sodden and stinking; face and hands, yellow. Waste chemicals from the munitions factory had got into the sewage system and gassed him when he went down to inspect. My company did not pause in its march, and I had only a glimpse of the group; but it reminded me so strongly of France that, but for the band music, I should have fainted.

Large drafts now frequently went off to the First, Second, Ninth and Tenth Battalions in France, and to the Eighth Battalion in Mesopotamia. Very few of the men warned for draft absented themselves. But they were always more cheerful about going in the spring and summer, when there was heavy fighting, than in the quieter winter months. (The regiment kept up its spirits even in the last year of the war. I was told that big drafts sent off during the critical weeks of the 1918 spring, when the Germans had broken through the Fifth Army, went down to the station singing and cheering enthusiastically. They might have been the reservists whom I had seen assembling at Wrexham on August 12th, 1914, to rejoin the Second Battalion just before it sailed for France.)

The day I joined the battalion from Osborne, I went via Liverpool Exchange Station and the electric railway to Litherland. Litherland Station was crowded with troops. I saw a well-remembered First Battalion face—D.C.M. and rosette, Médaille Militaire, Military Medal, no stripe. 'Lost them again, Sergeant Dickens?' I asked.

He grinned. 'Easy come, easy go, sir.'

Then the train came in, and I stretched out my hand with 'Good Luck!'

'You'll excuse us, sir,' said Dickens.

The draft shouted with laughter, and I saw why my hand had not been wrung, and also why the cheers had been so loud. Everyone of them was in handcuffs. They had been detailed a fortnight before for a draft in Mesopotamia, but wanted to get back to the First Battalion, so they overstayed their leave. The colonel, not understanding the situation, put them into the guardroom to make sure of them for the next draft. They were now going back in handcuffs, under an escort of military police, to the battalion of their choice. The men bore the colonel no ill-will for the handcuffs. A good-hearted man, he took a personal interest in the camp kitchen, had built a cinema-hut within the camp, been reasonably mild in Orderly Room, and done his best not to drive returned soldiers too hard.

I decided to leave Litherland somehow, forewarned what the winter would be like, with the mist steaming up from the Mersey and hanging about the camp, full of T.N.T. fumes. During the previous winter I used to sit in my hut, and cough and cough until I was sick. The fumes tarnished buttons and cap-badges, and made our eyes smart. I thought of going back to France, but realized the absurdity of the notion. Since 1916, the fear of gas had obsessed me: any unusual smell, even a sudden strong scent of flowers in a garden, was enough to send me trembling. And I couldn't face the sound of heavy shelling now; the noise of a car back-firing would send me flat on my face, or running for cover. But what about Palestine, where gas was unknown and shell-fire inconsiderable by comparison with France?

At my next medical board I asked to be passed in the category of B2, which meant: 'Fit for garrison service at home.' I reckoned on being sent to the Third Garrison Battalion of the regiment, now under canvas at Oswestry in Wales. From there, when I felt a bit better, I would get myself passed B1, or: 'Fit for garrison service abroad', and would, in due course, be sent to a Royal Welch garrison battalion in Egypt. Once there, it should be easy to get passed A1 and join the Twenty-fourth or Twenty-fifth (New Army) Battalion in Palestine.

So presently I was sent to Oswestry. We had a good colonel,

but the men were mostly compulsory enlistments; and the officers, with few exceptions, useless. My first task on arrival was to superintend the entraining of battalion stores and transport; we were moving to Kinmel Park Camp, near Rhyl. The adjutant gave me one hundred and fifty men, and allowed me six hours for the job. I chose fifty of the stronger men and three or four N.C.O.s who looked capable, then sent the remainder away to play football. By organizing the mob in First Battalion style, I got my fifty men to load the train in two hours less than the scheduled time. The colonel congratulated me. At Rhyl, he gave me the job of giving 'further instruction' to the sixty or so young officers sent to him from the cadet-battalions. Few officers in the battalion had seen any active service.

It was at this point that I remembered Nancy Nicholson. I had first met her in April, 1916, at the Nicholsons' Harlech house, while on leave after the operation on my nose. She was sixteen at the time, on holiday from school, and I knew her brother Ben, the painter, whose asthma kept him out of the Army. When I returned to France in 1917, I had called on Ben and the rest of the family in Chelsea, and the last person to say goodbye to me on the way to Victoria Station was Nancy. I remembered her standing in the doorway, in a black velvet dress with a coral necklace. She was of independent mind, good-natured, and as sensible about the war as anybody at home could be. In the summer of 1917, I had taken her to a musical review, the first review of my life.

I began a correspondence with Nancy, about some children's rhymes of mine which she wanted to illustrate. Soon I fell in love with her. On my next leave, in October 1917, I visited her at the farm where she worked in Huntingdonshire. Our letters became more intimate after this. She warned me that she was a feminist and that I had to be careful what I said about women; the attitude of the Huntingdon farmers to their wives and daughters kept her in a continual state of anger.

I had been passed B1 now, but the orders that came for me to proceed to Gibraltar upset my plans. Gibraltar being a dead-end, it would be as difficult to get from there to Palestine as it would from England. A friend in the War Office undertook to cancel the order until a vacancy could be found for me in the battalion stationed at Cairo. At Rhyl, I was enjoying my first independent command. I got it because of a rumoured invasion of the north-east coast, to follow a sortie of the German fleet. A number of battalions were sent across England for its defence. All fit men of the Third Garrison Battalion were ordered to move at twenty-four hours' notice to York. A slight error occurred, however, in the Morse message from War Office to Western Command. Instead of dash-dot-dash-dash, they sent dash-dot-dash-dot, so the battalion was sent to Cork instead; where, on second thoughts, it seemed just as much needed as in York—so there it stayed for the remainder of the war.

Ireland had been seething since the Easter Rebellion in 1916, and Irish troops at the depôts were now giving away their rifles to the Sinn Feiners. On getting these orders, the colonel told me that I was the only officer he could trust to look after the rest of the battalion—thirty young officers, four or five hundred crocks engaged in camp duties, and a draft of two hundred trained men under orders for Gibraltar. He left me a competent adjutant, and three officers' chargers to ride, also asking me to keep an eye on his children, whom he had to leave behind until a house could be found for them at Cork; I had been playing with them a good deal. I got the draft off all right, and their soldierlike appearance so impressed the inspecting general that he sent them all to the camp cinema at his own expense. This gave me another good mark with the colonel in Ireland. The climax of my faithful service was when I checked an attempt on the part of the camp quartermaster to make our battalion responsible for the loss of five hundred blankets.

I saw Nancy again when I visited London in December, and we decided to get married at once. Though attaching no importance to the ceremony, Nancy did not want to disappoint her father, who liked weddings and parties. I was still expecting orders for Egypt, and intended to go on from there to Palestine. However, Nancy's mother made it a condition of marriage—Nancy being still a minor—that I should visit a London lung-specialist to find out whether I would be fit for active service in the course of the next year or two. I went to Sir James Fowler, who had visited me at Rouen when I was wounded. He told me that my lungs were healthy enough, though I had bronchial adhesions and my wounded lung had only a third of its proper expansion; but that my general nervous condition made it folly for me to think of active service in any theatre of war.

Nancy and I were married in January, 1918, at St James's Church, Piccadilly. She was just eighteen, and I twenty-two. George Mallory acted as the best man. Nancy had read the marriage service for the first time that morning, and been so horrified that she all but refused to go through with the wedding, though I had arranged for the ceremony to be modified and reduced to the shortest possible form. Another caricature scene to look back on: myself striding up the red carpet, wearing field-boots, spurs and sword; Nancy meeting me in a blue-check silk wedding-dress, utterly furious; packed benches on either side of the church, full of relatives; aunts using handkerchiefs; the choir boys out of tune; Nancy savagely muttering the responses, myself shouting them in a parade-ground voice.

A week later, Nancy returned to her farm, and I to my command at Kinmel Park. It was an idle life now. No men attended parade; all were employed on camp duties. And I found a lieutenant with enough experience to attend to the 'further instruction' of the young officers. My Orderly Room took about ten minutes each day; crime was rare, and the adjutant always kept ready and in order the few documents to be signed; which left me free to ride all my three chargers over the countryside, in turn, for the rest of the day.

Wearying of this idleness at last, I arranged to be transferred to the Sixteenth Officer Cadet Battalion in another part of the same camp. There I did the same sort of work as with the Fourth at Oxford, and stayed from February 1918 until the Armistice on November 11th. Rhyl being much healthier than Oxford, I could play games without danger of another breakdown. Nancy got a job at a market-gardener's near the camp, and came up to live with me. A month or two later she found that she was having a baby, stopped land work, and went back to her drawing.

16

IN the middle of December the cadet battalions were wound
up, and the officers, after a few days' leave, sent back to their
units. I had orders to rejoin the Royal Welch Third Battalion,
now at the Castle Barracks, Limerick, but decided to overstay
my leave until the baby was born. Nancy expected it early in
January 1919, and her father took a house at Hove for the
occasion. Jenny, born on Twelfth Night, was not affected by
the shocks of the previous months. I went over to Limerick,
and there lied my way out of the overstaying of leave.

Limerick being a Sinn Fein stronghold, constant clashes
occurred between the troops and the young men of the town,
yet little ill-feeling; Welsh and Irish always got on well
together, just as Welsh and Scottish were sure to disagree.
The Royal Welch had the situation comfortably in hand;
they made a joke of politics and turned their entrenching-tool
handles into shillelaghs. Limerick looked like a war-ravaged
town. The main streets were pitted with holes like shell-
craters and many of the bigger houses seemed on the point of
collapse. Old Reilly at the antique shop, who remembered my
grandfather well, told me nobody built new houses at Limerick now; the birth-rate was declining and when one fell down
the survivors moved into another. He also said that everyone
died of drink in Limerick except the Plymouth Brethren.

Life did not start in the town before nine in the morning. Once, at about that time, I walked down O'Connell Street, formerly King George Street, and found it deserted. When the hour chimed, the door of a magnificent Georgian house flew open and out came, first a shower of slops, which just missed me, then a dog, then a nearly naked girl-child, who sat down in the gutter and rummaged in a heap of refuse for filthy pieces of bread; finally a donkey, which began to bray. I had pictured Ireland exactly so, and felt its charms as dangerous. When detailed to search for concealed rifles at the head of a task force, in a neighbouring village, I asked Attwater, the adjutant, to find a substitute. I explained that as an Irishman I did not care to be mixed up in Irish politics. That January I played my last game of rugger: as full back for the battalion against Limerick City. We were all crocks and our opponents seemed bent on showing what fine fighting material England had lost by withholding Home Rule. How jovially they jumped on me, and rubbed my face in the mud!

My new loyalty to Nancy and Jenny tended to overshadow regimental loyalty, now that the war seemed to be over. I decided to resign my commission at once. Consulting the priority list of trades for demobilization, I found that agricultural workers and students were among the first classes to go. I did not particularly want to be a student again and would rather have been an agricultural worker—Nancy and I had spoken of farming when the war ended—but where was my agricultural background? And I could take a two years' course at Oxford with a Government grant of two hundred pounds a year, and be excused the intermediate examination on account of war-service. The preliminary examination I had already been excused because of a 'higher certificate examination' passed at Charterhouse; so there remained only the finals. The grant would be increased by a children's allowance. It seemed absurd at the time to suppose that university degrees would count for anything in a regenerated post-war England; but Oxford offered itself as a convenient place to mark time until I felt more like earning a livelihood. We were all accustomed to the wartime view, that the sole qualification for peacetime employment would be a good record of service in the field, that we expected our scars and our commanding officers' testimonials to get us whatever we wanted. A few of my fellow-officers did manage, as a matter of fact, to take advantage of the employers' patriotic spirit before it cooled again; sliding into jobs for which they were not properly qualified.

I wrote to a friend in the War Office Demobilization Department, asking him to hurry through my release. He wrote back that he would do his best, but that I must not have had charge of Government moneys for the past six months. As it happened, I had not at the time; but Attwater suddenly decided to put me in command of a company. He complained of being disastrously short of officers who could be trusted with company accounts. The latest arrivals from the New Army battalions were a constant shame to the senior officers. Paternity-orders, dud cheques, and drunkenness on parade grew frequent; not to mention table manners at which the mess-sergeant stood aghast. We now had two mess ante-rooms, the junior and the senior; yet if a junior officer happened to be regimentally a gentleman (belonged, that is, to the North Wales landed gentry, or came from Sandhurst) the colonel invited him to use the senior ante-room and mix with his own class. The situation must have seemed very strange to the three line-battalion second-lieutenants captured at Mons in 1914, now promoted captains by the death of most of their contemporaries and set free by the terms of the Armistice.

Attwater cancelled the intended appointment only when I promised to help him with the battalion theatricals now being arranged for St David's Day; I undertook to play Cinna in

Julius Caesar. His change of mind saved me over two hundred pounds, because next day the senior lieutenant of the company which I was to have taken over went off with the cash-box, and I should have been legally responsible for its loss. Before the war he used to give displays on Blackpool Pier as 'The Handcuff King'. He got away safely to the United States.

I rode out a few miles from Limerick to visit my uncle, Robert Cooper, at Cooper's Hill. He was a farmer, a retired naval commander, and the Sinn Feiners had begun burning his ricks and driving his cattle. Through the window he showed me distant herds grazing beside the Shannon. 'They have been there all winter,' he said despondently, 'but I haven't had the heart to take a look at them these three months.' I spent the night at Cooper's Hill, and woke up with a sudden chill, which I recognized as the first symptoms of Spanish influenza.

Back at the barracks, I found that a War Office telegram had come through for my demobilization, but that all demobilization among troops in Ireland was to be stopped on the following day for an indefinite period because of the Troubles. Attwater, showing me the telegram, said: 'We're not going to let you go. You promised to help with those theatricals.' I protested; he stood firm; but I did not intend to have influenza at an Irish military hospital with my lungs in their present condition.

I decided to make a run for it. The orderly-room sergeant had made out my papers on receipt of the telegram; all my kit lay ready packed. There remained only two things to get: the commanding officer's signature to the statement that I had handled no company moneys, and the secret code-marks which the battalion demobilization officer alone could supply —but he was hand-in-glove with Attwater, so I dared not ask him for them. The last train before demobilization ended would be the six-fifteen from Limerick that same evening, February 13th. My one hope was to wait until Attwater left the Orderly Room and then casually ask the commanding officer to sign the statement, without mentioning Attwater's objection to my going. Attwater remained in the Orderly Room until five minutes past six. As soon as he was out of sight I hurried in, saluted, got the necessary signature—fortunately my old friend Macartney-Filgate was now in command—saluted again, and hurried away to collect my baggage. I had counted on a jaunting-car at the barrack gates but found none. About five minutes left, and the station a good distance away! A First Battalion corporal passed. I shouted to him: 'Corporal Summers, quick! Get a squad of men! I've *got my ticket* and must catch the last train home.' Summers promptly called four men; they picked up my stuff and doubled off with it, left, right, left, to the station. I tumbled into the train as it moved slowly out and threw a pound-note to Corporal Summers. 'Goodbye, corporal, drink my health!'

Yet still I had not got my code-marks, and knew that when I reached the demobilization centre at Wimbledon the officers there would refuse to let me go. Not that I cared very much. I should at least have my influenza in an English, and not an Irish, hospital. My temperature was running high, and my mind working clearly, as it always does in fever, with its visual imagery, which is cloudy and partial at ordinary times, defined and complete. We reached Fishguard after a rough crossing. I bought a copy of the *South Wales Echo* and read that a strike of London Electric Railwaymen would take place the next day, February 14th, unless the railway directors met the union's demands. So as the train steamed into Paddington, I jumped out, fell down, picked myself up and ran across to the station entrance where, in spite of competition from porters—a feeble crew at this period—I seized the only taxi in sight as its occupant paid the fare. I had foreseen the taxi-shortage and could afford to waste no time. I brought my taxi back to the train, where scores of stranded officers eyed

128

me with envy. One, a fellow-traveller in my compartment, had been met by his wife. 'Excuse me,' I said, 'but would you like to share my taxi anywhere? (I have influenza, I warn you.) I'm going down to Wimbledon, so I shall be getting out at Waterloo; the steam-trains are still running.' That delighted them, because they lived at Ealing and had no idea how to get home except by taxi.

On the way to Waterloo he said: 'I wish there were some way of showing our gratitude—something we could do for you.'

'Well, there's only one thing in the world that I want at the moment. But you can't give it to me, I'm afraid. And that's the set of secret code-marks to complete my demobilization papers. I've bolted from Ireland without them, and there'll be hell to pay if the Wimbledon people send me back.'

He rapped on the glass of the taxi, told the driver to stop, got down his bag, opened it, and produced a satchel of army forms. 'Well,' he said, 'I happen to be the Cork District Demobilization officer, and here's the whole bag of tricks.'

Then he filled in my papers.

At Wimbledon, instead of having to wait in a queue for the expected nine or ten hours, I got released at once; Ireland was officially a 'theatre of war', and demobilization from theatres of war had priority over home-service demobilization. After a hurried visit to my parents, now back in our own house half a mile across the Common, I went on to Hove. Arriving at supper-time, I warned Nicholson about my influenza, and hurried away to bed. Within a day or two, the whole family caught it, except Nicholson, Jenny and the housemaid, a Welsh gipsy, who kept it off by charm—the leg of a lizard tied in a bag round her neck. A new epidemic, as bad as the summer one, had started; not a nurse could be found in all Brighton. Nicholson at last rounded up two ex-nurses: one competent, but frequently drunk, and with the habit, when drunk, of ransacking all the wardrobes in the house and piling the contents into her own bag. The other sober, but incompetent, would stand a dozen times a day in front of the open window, arms outspread, and cry in a stage-voice: 'Sea, sea, give my husband back to me!' The husband, by the way, was not drowned, merely unfaithful.

A doctor, found with equal difficulty, gave me no hope of recovery; it was septic pneumonia now, and had affected both my lungs. But, having come through the war, I refused to die of influenza. This made the third time in my life that I had been given up, and each time because of my lungs. I should have mentioned earlier in the book an attack of double-pneumonia following measles, which nearly did for me at the age of seven. Maggie, the gipsy-servant, wept whenever she dusted my room—I thought because of a tiff with her young man, but these were tears for me, my widow and my orphan girl. I focused attention on a poem, 'The Troll's Nosegay', which was giving me trouble; I had taken it through thirty drafts and still it would not come right. The thirty-fifth draft passed scrutiny, I felt better, and Maggie smiled again.

A few weeks later, I watched a mutiny of the Guards, when about a thousand men of all regiments marched out from Shoreham Camp and paraded through the Brighton streets, in protest against unnecessary restrictions. The troops' impatience of military discipline between the Armistice and the signing of peace delighted Siegfried Sassoon; he had taken a prominent part in the General Election which Lloyd George forced immediately after the Armistice, asking for a warrant to hang the Kaiser and make a stern peace. Siegfried, supporting Philip Snowden's candidature on a Pacifist platform, had faced a threatening civilian crowd; he trusted that his three wound-stripes and the mauve and white Military Cross ribbon would give him a privileged hearing. Snowden and Ramsay MacDonald were now perhaps the two most unpopular men in England, and whatever hopes we had nursed of a general anti-Government rising by ex-servicemen soon faded. Once back in England, they were content with a roof over their heads, civilian food, beer that was at least better than French beer, and enough blankets at night. Any overcrowding in their homes was as nothing compared to what they had grown accustomed to; a derelict French four-roomed cottage would provide billets for sixty men. Having won the war, they were satisfied and left the rest to Lloyd George. The only serious outbreak took place at Rhyl. There a two days' mutiny of young Canadians caused much destruction and several deaths. The signal for the rising was a cry: 'Come on, the Bolsheviks!'

Nancy, Jenny and I went up to Harlech, where Nicholson lent us his house to live in. We were there for a year. I discarded my uniform, having worn nothing else for four and a half years, and looked into my trunk to see what civilian clothes I still had. The one suit, other than school uniforms which I found, no longer fitted. The Harlech villagers treated me with the greatest respect. At the Peace Day celebrations in the castle, I was asked, as the senior Man of Harlech who had served overseas, to make a speech about the glorious dead. I spoke in commendation of the Welshman as a fighting man and earned loud cheers. But not only did I have no experience of independent civilian life, having gone straight from school into the Army: I was still mentally and nervously organized for war. Shells used to come bursting on my bed at midnight, even though Nancy shared it with me; strangers in daytime would assume the faces of friends who had been killed. When strong enough to climb the hill behind Harlech and revisit my favourite country, I could not help seeing it as a prospective battlefield. I would find myself working out tactical problems, planning how best to hold the Upper Artro Valley against an attack from the sea, or where to place a Lewis-gun if I were trying to rush Dolwreiddiog Farm from the brow of the hill, and what would be the best cover for my rifle-grenade section. I still had the Army habit of commandeering anything of uncertain ownership that I found lying about; also a difficulty in telling the truth—it was always easier for me now, when charged with any fault, to lie my way out in Army style. I applied the technique of taking over billets or trenches to a review of my present situation. Food, water supply, possible dangers, communication, sanitation, protection against the weather, fuel and light—I ticked off each item as satisfactory.

Other loose habits of wartime survived, such as stopping cars for a lift, talking without embarrassment to my fellow-travellers in railway carriages. Also, I retained the technique of endurance: a brutal persistence in seeing things through, somehow, anyhow, without finesse, satisfied with the main points of any situation. But at least I modified my unrestrainedly foul language. The greatest difficulty lay in facing the problem of money, which had not worried me since those first days at Wrexham; but at the moment my savings of some £150, my war-bonus of £250, the disability pension of £60 a year that I now drew, and occasional sums that came in from poems, seemed plenty. Nancy and I engaged a nurse and a general servant, and lived as though we had an income of a thousand a year. Nancy spent much of her time illustrating some poems of mine; I got my *Country Sentiment* in order, and wrote reviews.

Very thin, very nervous and with about four years' loss of sleep to make up, I was waiting until I got well enough to go to Oxford on the Government educational grant. I knew that it would be years before I could face anything but a quiet country life. My disabilities were many: I could not use a telephone, I felt sick every time I travelled by train, and to see more than two new people in a single day prevented me from sleeping. I felt ashamed of myself as a drag on Nancy, but had sworn on the very day of my demobilization never to be under anyone's orders for the rest of my life. Somehow I must live by writing.

Siegfried had gone to live at Oxford as soon as he was demobilized, expecting me to join him. However, after a couple of terms there, he accepted the literary editorship of the newly-published *Daily Herald*. He sent me books to review for it. In those days, the *Daily Herald* was not respectable, but violently anti-militarist and the only daily newspaper that dared protest against the Versailles Treaty and the blockade of Russia by the British fleet. The Treaty of Versailles shocked me; it seemed destined to cause another war some day, yet nobody cared.

The *Herald* spoiled our breakfast every morning. We read in it of unemployment all over the country due to the closing of munition factories; of ex-servicemen refused reinstatement in the jobs they had left when war broke out, of market-rigging, lock-outs, and abortive strikes. I began to hear news, too, of the penury to which my mother's relatives in Germany had been reduced, particularly the retired officials whose pensions, by the collapse of the mark, now amounted to only a few shillings a week. Nancy and I took all this to heart and called ourselves socialists.

My family, who were living permanently in Harlech, having sold the house at Wimbledon, did not know quite how to treat me. I had fought gallantly for my country—indeed, of six brothers, I alone had seen active service, and my shell-shocked state entitled me to every consideration; but my sympathy for the Russian rebellion against the corrupt Czarist Government outraged them. I once more forfeited the good will of my Uncle Charles. My father tried to talk me over, reminding me that my brother Philip, once a pro-Boer and a Fenian, had recovered from his youthful revolutionary idealism and come out all right in the end. Most of my elder brothers and sisters were in the Near East, either British officials, or married to British officials. My father hoped that when I recovered I would go to Egypt, perhaps in the consular service, where the family influence would help me, and there get over my 'revolutionary enthusiasm'.

Socialism with Nancy was a means to a single end: namely judicial equality between the sexes. She ascribed all the wrong in the world to male domination and narrowness, and would not see my experiences in the war as anything comparable with the sufferings that millions of working-class married women went through without complaint. This, at least, had the effect of putting the war into the background for me; my love for Nancy made me respect her views. But male stupidity and callousness became such an obsession with her that she began to include me in her universal condemnation of men. Soon she could not bear a newspaper in the house, for fear of reading some paragraph that would horrify her—about the necessity of keeping up the population; or about women's limited intelligence; or anything at all about women written by clergymen. She kept her own name for all purposes, refusing to be called 'Mrs Graves' in any circumstances. She explained that, as 'Mrs Graves', she had no personal validity. Children, at that time, were the sole property of the father; the mother not being legally a parent.

17

IN October, 1919, I went to Oxford at last, and Nicholson gave us the Harlech furniture to take along. Oxford was overcrowded; the lodging-house keepers, some of whom nearly starved during the war, now had their rooms booked up terms ahead, and charged accordingly. Keble College built a row of huts for its surplus students. Not an unfurnished house could be rented anywhere within the three-mile radius. I solved the difficulty by pleading ill-health and getting permission from St John's College to live five miles out, on Boar's Hill—where John Masefield, who thought well of my poetry, had offered to rent us a cottage at the bottom of his garden.

We found the University remarkably quiet. The returned soldiers did not feel tempted to rag about, break windows, get drunk, or have tussles with the police and races with the Proctors' 'bull-dogs', as in the old days. The boys straight from the public schools kept quiet too, having had war preached at them continually for four years, with orders to carry on loyally at home while their brothers served in the trenches, and make themselves worthy of such sacrifices. Since the boys went off to cadet-battalions at the age of seventeen, the masters kept firm control of the schools; trouble there nearly always came from the eighteen-year-olds. G. N. Clarke, a history don at Oriel, who had got his degree at Oxford just before the war and meanwhile been an infantry-man in France and a prisoner in Germany, told me: 'I can't make out my pupils at all. They are all "Yes, sir" and "No, sir". They seem positively to thirst for knowledge and scribble away in their notebooks like lunatics. I can't remember a single instance of such stern endeavour in pre-war days.'

The ex-servicemen, who included scores of captains, majors, colonels, and even a one-armed twenty-five-year-old briga-dier, insisted on their rights. At St John's, they formed a 'College Soviet', successfully demanded an entire revision of the scandalous catering system, and chose an undergraduate representative to sit on the kitchen committee. The elder dons, whom I had often seen during the war trembling in fear of an invasion, with the sacking and firing of the Oxford colleges and the rape of their families in the Woodstock and Banbury Roads, and who then regarded all soldiers, myself included, as their noble saviours, now recovered their pre-war self-possession and haughtiness. The change in their manner amused me. My moral tutor, however, though he no longer saluted me when we met, remained a friend; he persuaded the College to let me change my course from Classics to English Language and Literature, and take up my £60 Classical Exhibition notwithstanding. I felt glad now that it was only an exhibition, not a scholarship, though in 1913 this had disappointed me: College regulations permitted exhibitioners to be married; scholars must remain single.

I found the English Literature course tedious, especially the insistence on eighteenth-century poets. My tutor, Percy Simpson, the editor of Ben Jonson's plays, sympathized, telling me that he had suffered once, as a boy, for preferring the Romantic Revivalists. Yet he warned me not on any account to disparage the eighteenth century when I sat for my finals. I also found it difficult to concentrate on cases, genders and irregular verbs in Anglo-Saxon grammar. The Anglo-Saxon lecturer was candid about his subject: it was, he said, a language of purely linguistic interest, and hardly a line of Anglo-Saxon poetry extant possessed the slightest literary merit. I disagreed. I thought of Beowulf lying wrapped in a blanket among his platoon of drunken thanes in the Gothland billet; Judith going for a *promenade* to Holofernes's staff-tent; and *Brunanburgh* with its bayonet-and-cosh fighting—all this came far closer to most of us than the drawing-room and deer-park atmosphere of the eighteenth century. Edmund Blunden, who also had leave to live on Boar's Hill because of gassed lungs, was taking the same course. The war still continued for both of us, and we translated everything into trench-warfare terms. In the middle of a lecture I would have a sudden very clear experience of men on the march up the Béthune–La Bassée road; the men would be singing, while French children ran along beside us, calling out: 'Tommee, Tommee, give me bullee beef!' and I would smell the stench of the knacker's yard just outside the town. Or it would be in Laventie High Street, passing a company billet; an N.C.O. would roar: 'Party, 'shun!' and the Second Battalion men in shorts, with brown knees, and brown, expressionless faces, would spring to their feet from the broken steps where they were sitting. Or I would be in a barn with my first platoon of the Welsh Regiment, watching them play nap by the light of dirty candle stumps. Or in a deep dug-out at Cambrin, talking to a signaller; I would look up the shaft and see somebody's muddy legs coming down the steps; then there would be a sudden crash and the tobacco smoke in the dug-out would shake with the concussion and twist about in patterns like the marbling on books. These day-dreams persisted like an alternate life and did not leave me until well into 1928. The scenes were nearly always recollections of my first four months in France; the emotion-recording apparatus seemed to have failed after Loos.

The eighteenth century owed its unpopularity largely to its Frenchness. Anti-French feeling among most ex-soldiers amounted almost to an obsession. Edmund, shaking with nerves, used to say at this time: 'No more wars for me at any price! Except against the French. If there's ever a war with them, I'll go like a shot.' Pro-German feeling had been increasing. With the war over and the German armies beaten, we could give the German soldier credit for being the most efficient fighting-man in Europe. I often heard it said that only the blockade had beaten the Fritzes; that in Haig's last push they never really broke, and that their machine-gun sections held us up long enough to cover the withdrawal of the main forces. Some undergraduates even insisted that we had been fighting on the wrong side: our natural enemies were the French.

A number of poets were living on Boar's Hill; too many, Edmund and I agreed. It was now almost a tourist centre, dominated by Robert Bridges, the Poet Laureate, with his bright eye, abrupt challenging manner, and a flower in his buttonhole—one of the first men of letters to sign the Oxford recantation of wartime hatred against the Germans.

I saw most of John Masefield, a nervous, generous, correct man, very sensitive to criticism, who seemed to have suffered greatly in the war, as an orderly in a Red Cross unit; he was now working on *Reynard the Fox*. He wrote in a hut in his garden, surrounded by tall gorse-bushes, and only appeared at meal-times. In the evening he used to read his day's work over to Mrs Masefield, and they corrected it together. Masefield being at the height of his reputation at the time, a constant stream of American visitors washed against his door. Mrs Masefield protected 'Jan'. She came from the north of Ireland, and put a necessary brake on Jan's generosity and sociability. We admired her careful housekeeping, and the way she stood up for her rights where less resolute people would have shrunk. As an example: some neighbours of ours had a particularly stupid Airedale; they were taking it for a walk when a wild rabbit ran across the road from the Masefield's gorse plantation.

The Airedale dashed at the rabbit, and missed as usual. The rabbit, not giving sufficient credit for stupidity and slowness, doubled back, but found the dog not yet recovered from its mistake and ran right into its open jaws. The dog's owners, delighted at the brilliant performance of their pet, retrieved the rabbit, which was a small and inexperienced one, and took it home for the pot. Mrs Masefield had been watching through the plantation fence. This not being, strictly, a public road, the rabbit was legally hers. That evening, they heard a knock at the door. 'Come in, oh, do come in, Mrs Masefield!' She had called to demand the skin of her rabbit. Mrs Masefield's one extravagance was bridge; she used to play at a halfpenny a hundred, to steady her play. But she was a considerate land-lord to us.

In March our second child arrived and we called him David. Nancy was determined to have four children; they were to resemble the children in her drawings, and be girl, boy, girl, boy, in that order. She intended to get it all over with quickly; she believed in young parents with families of three or four children fairly close together in age. She had her way exactly, but began to regret her marriage, as a breach of faith with herself—a concession to patriarchy. She wanted somehow to be dis-married—not by divorce, which was as bad as marriage —so that she and I could live together without any legal or religious obligation to do so.

18

THE first time I met Colonel T. E. Lawrence, he happened to be wearing full evening dress. That must have been in February or March 1920, and the occasion was a guest-night at All Souls', where he had been awarded a seven-years' Fellowship. The formality of evening dress concentrates attention on eyes, and Lawrence's eyes immediately held me. They were startlingly blue, even by artificial light, and never met the eyes of the person he addressed, but flickered up and down as though making an inventory of clothes and limbs. Lawrence had not long finished with the Peace Conference, where he acted as adviser to the Emir Feisal, and was now tinkering at the second draft of *The Seven Pillars of Wisdom*, his Fellowship having been granted him on condition that he wrote the book as a formal history of the Arab Revolt.

I used to visit his rooms in the mornings between lectures, but not before eleven o'clock or half past, because he worked by night, going to bed at dawn. Lawrence's rooms were dark and oak-panelled, with a large table and a desk as the principal furniture. There were also two heavy leather chairs, simply acquired. An American oil-financier had come in suddenly one day when I was there and said: 'I am here from the States, Colonel Lawrence, to ask a single question. You are the only man who will answer it honestly. Do Middle-Eastern conditions justify my putting any money in South Arabian oil?'

Lawrence, without rising, quietly answered: 'No.'

'That's all I wanted to know; it was worth coming for. Thank you, and good day!' In his brief glance about the room he missed something and, on his way home through London, chose the chairs and had them sent to Lawrence with his card.

I knew nothing definite of Lawrence's wartime activities, though my brother Philip had been with him in the Intelligence Department at Cairo in 1915, making out the Turkish Order of Battle. I did not question him about the Revolt, partly because he seemed to dislike the subject and partly because of a convention between him and me that the war should not be mentioned: we were both suffering from its effects and enjoying Oxford as a too-good-to-be-true relaxation. Thus, though the long, closely-written foolscap sheets of *The Seven Pillars* were always stacked in a neat pile on his living-room table, I restrained my curiosity. He occasionally spoke of his archaeological work in Mesopotamia before the war; but poetry, especially modern poetry, was what we discussed most.

He wanted to meet what poets there were, and through me came to know, among others, Siegfried Sassoon, Edmund Blunden, Masefield and, later, Thomas Hardy. He frankly envied poets. He felt that they had some sort of secret which he might be able to grasp and profit from. He envisaged the poets' secret as a technical mastery of words rather than as a particular mode of living and thinking. I had not yet learned enough to be able to dispute this, and when I did begin to learn, some years later, found Lawrence difficult to convince. To him, painting, sculpture, music and poetry were parallel activities, differing only in the medium used.

Lawrence behaved very much like an undergraduate at times. One day I happened to visit the top of the Radcliffe Camera and look down on the roofs of neighbouring colleges.

From a pinnacle of All Souls' fluttered a small crimson Hedjaz flag: Lawrence had been a famous roof-climber when up at Jesus College twelve years before this. He told me of two or three schemes for brightening All Souls' and Oxford generally. One was for improving the rotten turf in the Quadrangle; he had suggested at a College meeting that it should be manured or replaced; no action was taken. He now proposed to plant mushrooms on it, so that they would be forced to returf the whole extent; and he consulted a mushroom expert in town. But the technical difficulties of mushroom culture proved to be great, and Lawrence went away to help Winston Churchill with the Middle-Eastern settlement of 1922 before they could be overcome.

At this time I had little to do with the children; they were in the hands of Nancy and the nurse. Nancy felt that she needed some activity besides drawing, but could not decide what. One evening, in the middle of the long vacation, she suddenly said: 'I must get away out of all this at once. Boar's Hill stifles me. Let's go off on bicycles somewhere.'

We packed a few things and rode off in the general direction of Devon. The nights were coldish and, not having brought any blankets, we cycled by night and slept by day. We rode across Salisbury Plain in the moonlight, passing Stonehenge and several deserted army camps which had an even more ghostly look. They could provide accommodation for a million men: the number of men killed in the British and Overseas Forces during the war. Finding ourselves near Dorchester, we turned aside to visit Thomas Hardy, whom we had met not long before when he came to get his honorary doctor's degree at Oxford. Hardy was active and gay, with none of the aphasia and wandering of attention that we had noticed in him there.

After tea with him in his garden, he asked to see some of my new poems. I fetched him one.

'Do you write easily?' he inquired.

'This poem is in its sixth draft and will probably be finished in two more.'

'Why!' he said, 'I have never in my life taken more than three or perhaps four, drafts for a poem. I am afraid of it losing its freshness.'

He said that he could once sit down and write novels by a time-table, but that poetry always came to him by accident, which perhaps was why he prized it more highly.

He spoke disparagingly of his novels, though admitting that he had enjoyed writing certain chapters. As we walked around the garden, Hardy paused at a spot near the greenhouse. He had once been pruning a tree here when an idea for a story suddenly entered his head. The best story he had ever conceived, and it came complete with characters, setting, and even some of the dialogue. But not having pencil or paper with him, and wanting to finish his pruning before the weather broke, he took no notes. By the time he sat down at his table to recall the story, all was utterly gone. 'Always carry a pencil and paper,' he said, adding: 'Of course, even if I remembered that story now, I couldn't write it. I'm past novel-writing. But I often wonder what it can have been.'

He regarded professional critics as parasites, no less noxious than autograph-hunters, wished the world rid of them, and also regretted having listened to them as a young man; on their advice he had cut out from his early poems dialect-words which possessed no ordinary English equivalents.

We left the next day, after another of Hardy's attacks on the critics at breakfast. He complained that they accused him of pessimism. One critic singled out as an example of gloom his poem on the woman whose house burned down on her wedding night. 'Of course it's a humorous piece,' said Hardy, 'and the man must have been thick-witted not to see that. On reading his criticism, I went through my last collection of poems with a pencil, marking them S, N and C according as they were sad, neutral or cheerful. I found them in pretty well equal proportions; which nobody could call pessimism.' Of his own poems he told me that, once written, he cared very little what happened to them.

From Dorchester we cycled to Tiverton in Devon, where Nancy's old nurse kept a fancy-goods shop. Nancy helped her dress the shop-window, and advised her about framing the prints which she was selling. She also gave the shop a good turn-out, dusted the stock, and took her turn behind the counter. As a result of Nancy's work, the week's receipts went up several shillings and continued at the improved figure for a week or two after we were gone. This gave Nancy the idea of starting a shop herself on Boar's Hill, a large residential district with no shop nearer than three miles away. We could buy a second-hand army hut, stock it with confectionery, groceries, tobacco, hardware, medicines, and all the other things that one finds in a village shop, run it tidily and economically, and make our fortune. I promised to help her while the vacation lasted.

But army huts could not be bought at any reasonable price (the timber-merchants were in a ring); so a local carpenter built a shop to Nancy's design. A neighbour rented us a corner of his field close to the road. The work got finished in good time, and we bought the stock. The *Daily Mirror* advertised the opening on its front page with the heading 'SHOP-KEEPING ON PARNASSUS', and crowds came up from Oxford to look at us. We soon began to realize that it must either be a large general shop which made Boar's Hill more or less independent of Oxford (and of the unsatisfactory system of vans calling at the door and bringing inferior foods with 'take it or leave it'), or a small sweet and tobacco shop that offered no challenge to the Oxford tradesmen. We decided on the challenge. The building had to be enlarged, and two or three hundred pounds' worth of stock purchased. I used to serve in the shop several hours of the day, while Nancy went round to the big houses for the daily orders.

Term had now begun, and I should have been attending lectures in Oxford. Another caricature scene: myself, wearing a green-baize apron this time, with flushed face and disordered hair, selling a packet of Bird's Eye tobacco to the Poet Laureate with one hand, and with the other weighing out half a pound of brown sugar for Sir Arthur Evans's gardener's wife.

Finally, the shop business ousted everything, not only Nancy's painting but my University work, and Nancy's proper supervision of the house and children. We engaged a boy to call for orders, and soon had the custom of every resident on Boar's Hill, except two or three. Even Mrs Masefield used to visit us once a week. She always bought the same tin of sink-powder and packet of soap-flakes, paying money down from a cash-box which she carried with her. The moral problems of trade interested me. Nancy and I both found it very difficult at this time of fluctuating prices to be really honest; we could not resist the temptation of under-charging the poor villagers of Wootton, who were frequent customers, and recovering our money from the richer residents. Playing at Robin Hood came easily to me. Nobody ever detected the fraud; it was as easy as shelling peas, the boy said, who also took his turn behind the counter. We found that most people bought tea by price and not by quality. If we happened to be out of the tea, selling at ninepence a quarter, which Mrs So-and-so always bought, refusing the eightpenny tea, and if Mrs So-and-so asked for it in a hurry, we used to make up a pound of sevenpenny, which was the same colour as the ninepenny, and charge it at ninepence. The difference would not be noticed.

We felt sorry for commercial travellers who sweated up the hill with their heavy bags of samples, usually on foot, and had to be sent away without any orders. They would pitch a hard-luck tale, and often we relented and got in more stock than we needed. In gratitude they would tell us some of the tricks of the trade, advising us, for instance, never to cut cheese or bacon exactly to weight, but to make it an ounce or two more and overcharge for this extra piece. 'There's few can do the sum before you take the stuff off the scales, and there's fewer still who take the trouble to weigh up again when they get back home.'

The shop lasted six months. Prices began falling at the rate of about five per cent every week, the stock on our shelves had depreciated greatly in value, we had let several of the Wootton villagers run up bad debts. Then I went down with influenza, at the same time as Nancy quarrelled with the nurse and had to take the house and children herself. When we came to reckon things up, we decided to cut our losses; hoping to recoup the original expenditure, and even to be in pocket on the whole transaction, by selling the shop and goodwill to a large firm of Oxford grocers who wished to buy it as a branch establishment. Unfortunately, however, the site was not ours, and Mrs Masefield prevailed on the landlord not to let any ordinary business firm take over the shop from us, and thus spoil local amenities. No other site being available, we had to sell off what stock remained at bankruptcy prices to the wholesalers, and find a buyer for the building. Unfortunately again, the building was not made in bolted sections to be re-erected elsewhere; it could be sold only as timber, and during these six months the corner in timber had also been broken and prices had fallen steeply. We recovered twenty pounds of the two hundred that had been spent on it, but were some five hundred pounds in debt to the wholesalers and others. A lawyer took everything in hand for us, and disposed of our assets; finally reducing the debt to some three hundred pounds. Nicholson sent Nancy a hundred-pound note (in a match-box) as his contribution, and Lawrence unexpectedly contributed the remainder. He gave me four chapters of *The Seven Pillars of Wisdom*, to sell for serial publication in the United States. As a point of honour, Lawrence refused to make any money out of the Revolt, even in the most indirect way; but if it could help a poet in difficulties, he saw no harm in that.

We gave the Masefields notice that the cottage would be free by the end of the June quarter 1921; but did not have any idea where to go, or what to do next. It seemed clear that we must get another cottage somewhere, live quietly, look after the children ourselves, and try to make what money we needed by writing and drawing. Nancy, who had taken charge of everything while I was ill, now set me the task of getting the cottage. It must be found in three weeks' time.

I protested: 'But you know there isn't a single cottage for rent anywhere.'

'Yes, but we simply *have* to get one.'

'All right, then, describe it in detail. Since there are no cottages, we might as well get a no-cottage that we really like.'

'Well, it must have six rooms, water indoors, a beamed attic, a walled-in garden, and it must be near the river. It must be in a village with shops, and yet a little removed from the village. The village must lie five or six miles from Oxford in the opposite direction from Boar's Hill. The church must have a tower and not a spire—I've always hated spires. And we can afford only ten shillings a week unfurnished.'

I took down other details about soil, sanitation, windows, stairs and kitchen sinks; laid a ruler across the Oxford ordnance map, and found five riverside villages which corresponded in general direction and distance with Nancy's stipulation. Of these five villages, two proved on inquiry to possess shops; and, of these two, one had a towered church and the other a spired church.

I went to a firm of house-agents in Oxford and asked: 'Have you any cottages to let unfurnished?'

The clerk laughed politely. 'What I want is a cottage just outside the village of Islip, with a walled garden, six rooms, water in the house, a beamed attic, and at a rent of ten shillings a week.'

'Oh, you mean the World's End cottage? But that's for sale, not for rent. However, it's failed to find a buyer for two years, so perhaps the owner will let it go now at five hundred pounds, which is only half of what he originally asked.'

The next day Nancy came to Islip with me. She looked around and said: 'Yes, this is the cottage all right, but I shall have to cut down the cypress trees, and change those window-panes. We'll move in on quarter-day.'

'But the money! We haven't the money.'

Nancy answered: 'If we could find the exact house, surely we can find a mere lump of money?'

She was right. My mother very kindly bought the cottage for five hundred pounds and let it to us at ten shillings a week.

19

My mother, in letting us the Islip house, put a clause in the agreement that it must be used as a residence only, and not for the carrying on of any trade or business. She wanted to guard herself against any further commercial enterprise on our part; but need not have worried—we had learned our lesson. Islip, an agricultural village, lay far enough from Oxford not to be contaminated by the roguery for which the outskirts of most university towns are notorious. The village policeman led an easy life. During the four years we lived there nothing of ours was ever stolen, and no Islip cottager cheated or offended us. Once, by mistake, I left my bicycle at the station for two days and, when I recovered it, not only were both lamps, the pump and the repair outfit still in place, but an anonymous friend had even cleaned it.

Every Saturday during the winter months I played football for the village team. We ex-soldiers reintroduced the game at Islip after a lapse of some eighty years. The village nonagenarian complained that football was not so manly now as in his boyhood. He pointed across the fields to a couple of aged willow-trees: 'Them used to be our home goals,' he said. 'T'other pair stood half a mile upstream. Constable stopped our play in the end. Three men were killed in the last game—

one kicked to death; t'other two drowned each other in a scrimmage. Her was a grand game.' I found Islip football, though not unmanly, ladylike by comparison with the Charterhouse game. When playing centre-forward, I often got booed for charging the goalkeeper as he fumbled with the shot he had saved. The cheers were reserved for my inside-left, who spent most of his time stylishly dribbling the ball in circles round and round the field until robbed of it; he seldom went anywhere near the goal. But the football club was democratic, unlike the cricket club. I played cricket the first season, but resigned because the team seldom consisted of the best eleven men available; regular players would be dropped to make room for visiting gentry.

Nancy and I did all the work ourselves, including the washing. I undertook the cooking; she made and mended the children's clothes; we shared the other chores. Catherine was born in 1922, and Sam in 1924. By the end of 1925, we had lived for eight successive years in an atmosphere of teething, minor accidents, epidemics, and perpetual washing of babies' napkins. I did not dislike this sort of life, except for the money difficulties and almost never getting away to London. 'Love in a cottage, I'm afraid,' had been the prophetic phrase current at our wedding. The strain told on Nancy, who was constantly ill, and I often had to take charge of everything. She tried to draw; but by the time she got her materials together some alarm from the nursery would always disturb her. At last she decided not to start again until all the children were house-trained and old enough for school. I kept on with my work because the responsibility for making money rested with me, and because nothing has ever stopped me writing. Nancy and I kept the cottage clean in a routine that left us little leisure for anything else: we had accumulated a number of brass ornaments and utensils that needed polishing and our children wore five times as many clean dresses as the neighbours' children did.

I worked through constant interruptions. I could recognize the principal varieties of babies' screams: hunger, indigestion, wetness, pins, boredom, wanting to be played with; and learned to disregard all but the more important ones. Most of my prose books published in those four years betray the conditions under which I wrote: they are scrappy, not properly considered, and obviously written out of reach of a reference library. Poetry alone did not suffer. When working at a poem in my head, I went on doing my mechanical tasks in a trance until I had time to sit down and record it. At one period I could allow myself only half an hour's writing a day, and then had to scribble hard in an effort to disburden my mind—I never sat chewing a pen. My poetry-writing has always been a painful process of continual corrections, corrections on top of corrections, and persistent dissatisfaction.

The children were all healthy and gave us little trouble. Nancy had strong views about giving them no meat or tea but as much fruit as they wanted, putting them to bed early, making them rest in the afternoon. We did our best to avoid the mistakes of our own childhood; but when they went to the village school we could not protect them from formal religion, class snobbery, political prejudice, and mystifying fairy stories of the facts of sex. Islip seemed as good a place as any for the happy childhood that we wanted them to have. They had fields to play in, and animals all around, and play-fellows of their own age. The river was close and we could borrow a canoe. They even liked school.

The villagers called me 'The Captain'; otherwise I had few reminders of the war, except my yearly visit to the standing Medical Board. The Board continued for some years to recommend me for a disability pension. My particular disability was neurasthenia; the train journey and the first-class army railway-warrant filled out with my rank and regiment usually produced reminiscential neurasthenia by the time I reached the Board.

Ex-service men were continually coming to the door selling boot-laces and asking for cast-off shirts and socks. We always gave them a cup of tea and money. Islip was a convenient halt between the Chipping Norton and the Oxford workhouses. One day an out-of-work ex-serviceman, a steamroller driver by trade, called with his three children, including a baby. Their mother had recently died in childbirth. We felt very sorry for them, and Nancy offered to adopt the eldest child, Daisy, who was about thirteen years old and her father's greatest anxiety. She undertook to train Daisy in housework, so that she would be able later to go into service. The steam-rollerman shed tears of gratitude; and Daisy, a big, ugly girl, strong as a horse and toughened by her three years on the roads, seemed happy enough to be a member of the family. Nancy made her new clothes, we cleaned her, bought her shoes, and gave her a bedroom. The steamrollerman wanted Daisy to continue her education, which had been interrupted by their wanderings. But the schoolmistress put Daisy into the baby class, and the bigger girls used to tease her. In return, she pulled their hair and thumped them, and learned to hate school. After a while she grew homesick for the road.

'That was a good life,' she used to say. 'Dad and me and my brother and the baby. The baby was a blessing. When I fetched him along to the back doors I nearly always won something. 'Course, I was artful. If they tried to slam the door in my face, I used to put my foot in it and say: "This is my little orphan brother." Then I used to look around and any-thing I seen I used to ast for. I used to ast for a pram for the baby, if I seen an old one in a shed; and I'd get it, too. 'Course, we had a pram really, a good one, and then we'd sell the pram I'd won in the next town we come to. Good beggars alway ast for something particular, something they seen lying about. It's no good asting for food or money. I used to pick up a lot for my dad. I was a better beggar nor he was, he said. We used to go along together singing "On the Road to Anywhere". And there was always the Spikes to go to when the weather got bad. They was very good to us there. The Spike at Chippy Norton was our winter home. We used to go to the movies once a week there. We had fine grub at Chippy. We been all over the country: Wales, and Devonshire, right up to Scotland, but we always come back to Chippy.'

Nancy and I were shocked one day when a tramp came to the door and Daisy slammed it in his face and told him to 'clear out of it, Nosey, and don't poke your ugly mug into respectable people's houses.' She went on: 'I know you, Nosey Williams, you and your ex-service papers what you pinched from a bloke down in Salisbury, and them bigamy charges against you a-waiting down at Plymouth. Hop it now, quick, or I'll run for the cop!'

Daisy told us the true stories of many of the beggars we had befriended. 'There's not one decent man in ten among them bums,' she said. 'My dad's the only decent one of the lot. The reason most of them is on the road is the cops have something against them, so they has to keep moving. 'Course, my dad don't like the life; he took to it too late. And my mum was very respectable, too. She kept us clean. Most of them bums is lousy, with nasty diseases, and they keeps out of the Spike as much as they can, 'cause they don't like the carbolic baths.'

Daisy stayed with us for a whole winter. When spring came, and the roads dried, her father called for her again. He couldn't manage the little ones without her, he said. That was the last we saw of Daisy, though she wrote once from Chipping Norton asking us for money.

My Government grant and College Exhibition had ended at the time we moved to Islip. Peace brought a slump in the sale of poetry, and our total income, counting birthday and Christmas cheques from relatives, now amounted to one hundred and thirty pounds a year, of which perhaps half came from my writing. As Nancy reminded me, this meant fifty shillings a week, and some farm labourers at Islip, with more children than ourselves, earned only thirty shillings. They lived a much harder life than we did, and had no one to fall back on, in case of sudden illness or other emergency. We used to get holidays, too, at Harlech, when my mother would insist on paying the train-fare as well as giving us our board free. Thinking how difficult conditions were for the labourers' wives kept Nancy permanently depressed.

We still called ourselves socialists, and when a branch of the Parliamentary Labour Party was formed in the village, lent the cottage for its weekly meetings throughout the winter months. Islip, though a rich agricultural area, had a reputation for slut-farming. Mr Wise, a farm labourer, one of our members, once heckled a speaker in the Conservative interest about a protective duty imposed by the Conservative Government on dried currants. The speaker answered patronizingly: 'Well, surely a duty on Greek currants won't hurt you working men at Islip? You don't grow currants in these parts, do you?'

'No, sir,' replied Mr Wise, 'the farmers' main crop hereabouts is squitch.'

They persuaded me to stand for the parish council, of which I became a member for a year. I wish now I had taken records of the smothered antagonism at the council meetings. There were seven members, with three representatives of Labour and three Conservative representatives of the farmers and gentry; the chairman was a Liberal, whom we supported as a generous employer, and the only farmer for miles around with training at an agricultural college. He held the balance very fairly. The Council nearly came to blows over a proposed application to the District Council for the building of new cottages; many returned ex-soldiers who wanted to marry had nowhere to live with their wives. The Conservative members opposed this application, because it would mean a penny on the rates.

Then there was the question of getting a recreation ground for the village. The football team did not wish to be dependent on the generosity of a big farmer who rented it to us at a nominal fee. The Conservatives opposed this plan, again in the interest of the rates, and pointed out that shortly after the Armistice the village had turned down a recreation ground scheme, preferring to spend the memorial subscription money on a cenotaph. The Labour members replied that the vote was taken, as at the 1918 General Election, before the soldiers could return to express their views. Nasty innuendoes were then aimed at farmers who had stayed at home and made their pile, while their labourers fought and bled. The chairman calmed the antagonists. Another caricature scene: myself in corduroys and a rough frieze coat, sitting in the village schoolroom (this time with no 'Evils of Alcoholism' around the walls, but nature drawings and mounted natural history specimens instead), debating, as an Oxfordshire village elder, whether or not Farmer Tomkins could use a footpath across the allotments as a bridle-path—having first overturned the decayed stile which, I urged, disproved his right.

This association with the Labour Party severed our friendly relations with the village gentry, who had hitherto regarded us as in their camp. My mother had taken the trouble to call on the Rector when she viewed the property, and he later asked me to speak from the chancel steps of the village church at a War Memorial service. He suggested that I should read war-poems. But instead of Rupert Brooke on the glorious dead, I read some of the more painful poems by Sassoon and Wilfred Owen about men dying from gas-poisoning, and about buttocks of corpses bulging from the mud. I also suggested that the men who had died were not particularly virtuous or particularly wicked, but just average soldiers, and that the survivors should thank God they were alive, and do their best to avoid wars in the future. Though the Church party, apart from the liberal-minded Rector, professed to be scandalized, the ex-servicemen had not been too well treated on their return, and liked to be told that they stood on equal terms with the glorious dead. They were modest men: I noticed that though respecting the King's desire to wear their campaign medals on this occasion, they kept them buttoned up inside their coats.

The leading Labourite at Islip was William Beckley, senior. He bore an inherited title dating from the time of Oliver Cromwell: being always known as 'Fisher' Beckley. A direct ancestor, fishing one day on the Cherwell during the siege of Oxford, had ferried Cromwell himself and a body of Parliamentary troops over the river. In return, Cromwell granted him perpetual fishing-rights from Islip to the stretch of river where the Cherwell Hotel now stands. Some time in the 1870s, American weed was introduced into the river and net-fishing at last became impossible. Fisher Beckley turned agricultural labourer. His socialist views prevented him from getting employment in the village, so he daily trudged to a farm some miles away. But he was still 'Fisher' Beckley, and for us cottagers the most respected man in Islip.

My parents were most disappointed when, because of the shop crisis and my illness, I failed to take the B.A. degree at Oxford. But Sir Walter Raleigh, as head of the English School, allowed me to sit for the later degree of Bachelor of Letters, and present a written thesis on any subject I chose. I published a volume of poems every year from 1920 to 1925; after *The Pierglass*, which appeared in 1921, I made no attempt to please the ordinary reading public, and did not even flatter myself that I was conferring benefits on posterity; I had no reason to suppose that posterity would be more appreciative

156

than my contemporaries. I never wrote unless a poem pressed to be written.

When several of my friends died, a feeling of ill luck clouded this period. Islip had ceased to be a country refuge. I found myself resorting to the wartime technique of getting through things somehow, anyhow, in the hope that they would mend. Nancy's poor health led her to do less and less work. Our finances were improved by an allowance from her father that covered the extra expense of the new children—we now had two hundred pounds a year—but cottage life with four of them under six years old, and Nancy ill, showed signs of palling. I might have, after all, to take a teaching job. But for that I needed a degree; so I completed my thesis, which I published as *Poetic Unreason*, and handed it in, already printed, to the examining board. To my surprise, they accepted it, and now I had my B. Litt.'s degree. However, I did not want a preparatory or secondary school job, which would keep me away from home all day; Nancy could not bear having anyone else but myself and her taking care of the children. There seemed no solution to my problem.

Then the doctor told us that if Nancy wished to regain her health she must spend the winter in Egypt. Thus, the only appointment that could possibly meet the case would be an independent teaching job in Egypt, at a very high salary, and with little work to do. A week or two later (this is how things have always happened in emergencies) I was invited to offer myself as a candidate for the post of Professor of English Literature at the newly-founded Royal Egyptian University, Cairo. I had been recommended, I found out afterwards, by two or three influential men, among them Arnold Bennett, always a good friend to me, and the first critic who spoke out strongly for my poems in the daily Press; and Lawrence, who had known Lord Lloyd, then High Commissioner of Egypt, during the Arab Revolt. The salary, including the passage money, amounted to fourteen hundred pounds a year.

I fortified these recommendations with others: from my neighbour, Colonel John Buchan, afterwards Lord Tweedismuir, and from Mr Asquith, now the Earl of Oxford, who had taken a fatherly interest in me and often visited our cottage at Islip.

I got the appointment. The indirect proceeds from poem-writing can be enormously higher than the direct ones.

20

So, second-class, by P. & O. to Egypt, with a nurse for the children, new clothes in the new cabin-trunks, and a Morris-Oxford in the hold.

The ship touched at Gibraltar, where we disembarked, bought figs, and rode round the town; I remembered the cancelled War Office telegram and thought what a fool I had been to prefer Rhyl. Luckily, a P. & O. director, who happened to be aboard, persuaded the captain to take the ship within half a mile of Stromboli, then in eruption; by dusk in a hailstorm, with the lava hissing into the sea. At Port Said, a friend of my sister's helped us through the Customs; I still felt sea-sick, but knew that I was in the East because he began talking about Kipling. Then on to Cairo, looking out of the windows all the way, delighted at summer fields in January.

My sister-in-law advised us against the more exclusive residential suburb of Gizereh, where she lived, so with her assistance we rented a flat at Heliopolis, a few miles east of Cairo. We found the cost of living very high, this being the tourist season, but reduced the grocery bill by taking advantage of the more reasonable prices at the British Army Canteen, where I presented myself as an officer on the Pension List. Our two Sudanese servants, contrary to all warnings about the natives, were temperate, punctual, respectful, and never, to my knowledge, stole a thing beyond the remains of a single joint of mutton. It seemed queer, no longer looking after the children, or doing housework; and wonderful to have as much time as I needed for my work.

The University was founded by King Fuad, who wished to be known as a patron of the arts and sciences. The Cairo University before this one had been nationalistic in its policy and, because not staffed with European experts, or supported by the Government, soon came to an end. King Fuad's University began ambitiously: Faculties of Science, Medicine and Letters, and a full complement of highly-paid professors, few of them Egyptians. The Medicine and Science faculties were predominantly English, but the appointments to the Faculty of Letters had been made in the previous summer, when the British High Commissioner went on holiday; else he would no doubt have discountenanced them, as being predominantly French and Belgian. Only one of my colleagues could speak English, and none had any knowledge of Arabic; yet of the two hundred Egyptian students, mostly sons of rich merchants and landowners, fewer than twenty knew more than a smattering of French—just enough for shopping purposes in the elegant stores—though every one of them had learned English in the secondary schools. All official University correspondence was conducted in classical Arabic, which admits no word of later date than Mohammed's time—not that I should have noticed any neologisms myself. The 'very learned Sheikh' Graves, as I was there described, used to take his hand-outs to the post office for interpretation. My twelve or thirteen French colleagues were men of the highest academic distinction, but two or three English village-school-masters would have gladly undertaken their work at one-third of their salaries, and done it far better. The University building, a former harem-palace of the Khedive, was built in luscious French style with mirrors and gilding.

British officials at the Ministry of Education begged me to keep the British flag flying in the Faculty of Letters. I assented. Though I had not come to Egypt as an ambassador of Empire, it irked me to let the French indulge in semi-political activities at my expense. The Dean, M. Grégoire, was an authority on Slav poetry: tough, witty, and capable. He had acquired a certain slyness and adaptability during the war when, as a Belgian civilian in the German occupation, he edited an underground publication. The one-legged Professor of French Literature, a war hero, patronized me at first. I was his young friend, rather than his dear colleague. But when he learned that I also had bled in the cause of civilization and France, I became his most esteemed chum.

The Frenchmen lectured with the help of Arabic interpreters, which made neither for speed nor for accuracy. I should have delivered two lectures a week. The Dean, however, soon decided that if the students were ever to dispense with the interpreters, they must be given special instruction in French —and this reduced the time for lectures, so that he could allow me only one a week. That one was pandemonium. The students were not hostile, merely excitable and anxious to show their regard for me and liberty and Zaghlul Pasha and the well-being of Egypt—all at the same time. They obliged me to shout at the top of my loudest barrack-square voice, which I had learned to pitch high for greater carrying-power, in order to restore silence.

No text-books of any sort were available, the University Library having no English department; and it took months to get books through the French librarian. This was January, and the students faced an examination in May. They professed themselves anxious to master Shakespeare, Wordsworth, and Byron in that time. I had no desire to teach Wordsworth and Byron to anyone, and wished to protect Shakespeare from them. Deciding to lecture on the most rudimentary forms of literature possible, I chose the primitive ballad and its development into epic and the drama. I might at least, perhaps, teach them the meaning of the simpler literary terms. But though they had taken English for eight years or so in the schools, I could not count on their understanding half what I told them. Nobody, for instance, when I spoke of a ballad-maker singing to his harp, knew what a harp looked like. I told them that it was what Kind David played upon, and drew a picture on the blackboard; at which they shouted: 'Oh, *anur*!' I had myself seen a communal ballad-group in action at the hind legs of the Sphinx, while a gang of fellaheen cleared away the sand; one of the gang acted as chantey-man to keep the others moving. But my students thought it beneath their dignity to admit the existence of ballads in Egypt. The fellaheen did not exist, in their eyes, except as lazy and rather disgusting animals. Printed notes of my lectures, with which to prepare for the examinations, were much in demand. I asked the clerical staff of the faculty to duplicate some of them, but they were kept too busy by the French professors and in spite of promises never got the job done. My lectures soon degenerated into lecture-notes for lectures that could not be given—but, at any rate, I kept the students busy scribbling in their notebooks.

For some weeks I missed even my single weekly lecture, because the students went on strike. This was Ramadan, when they had to fast for a month between sunrise and sunset. Between sunset and sunrise they ate rather more than usual, to make up: a tax on the digestive processes which affected their nerves. The pretext for striking was the intensive French instruction; but really they wanted leisure to cram for the examination at home. Then the blind Professor of Arabic, one of the few Egyptians with fame as an orientalist, published a book calling attention to pre-Islamic sources of the Koran. His lectures demanded greater mental effort than any of the rest, so when the examinations were held, most students absented themselves from the Arabic paper on religious grounds. To an orthodox Moslem the Koran, since dictated by God to Mohammed, could have no pre-Islamic sources.

I came to know only two of my students fairly well: a Greek and a Turk. The Turk was rich, intelligent, good-natured, perhaps twenty years old, and twice took me for a drive to the pyramids in his motor car. He spoke both French and English fluently, being almost the only student (except for twelve who had attended a French Jesuit college) with this facility. He apologized one day for having to miss my next lecture: he was about to be married. I asked whether this would be the first or second part of the ceremony. He said: 'The first. I will not be allowed to see my wife's face, because her family is orthodox; that must wait until the second ceremony.' But his sister, he explained, had been at school with the girl and told him that she was pretty and a good sort; also, his father respected her father. When the second ceremony took place, he confessed to perfect satisfaction. I learned that the bridegroom seldom refused to accept the bride when she lifted her veil, though he had the right to do so, and she had a similar right. Usually, the couple contrived to meet before even the first ceremony. The girl would slip the man a note saying: 'I shall be at Maison Cicurel by the hat-counter about three-thirty tomorrow afternoon, if you want to know what I look like. It will be quite in order for me to lift my veil as I try on a hat. You can recognize me by my purple parasol.'

I inquired about the rights of Moslem women in Egypt. Apparently divorce was simple. The man had only to declare in the presence of a witness: 'I divorce you, I divorce you, I divorce you,' and that did it. On the other hand, she could recover her original dowry, plus the interest accrued on it during her married life. Dowries were always heavy and divorces comparatively rare. The gentry considered it very low-class to keep more than one wife, unless she behaved so badly that her husband decided to shame her by taking another. I heard of an Egyptian who got angry with his wife one morning because the breakfast coffee came in cold. He shouted: 'I divorce you, I divorce you, I divorce you!'

'Oh, my dear,' she exclaimed, 'now you've done it! The servants heard what you said. I must go back to my father with my ten thousand pounds and my sixty camels.'

He apologized for his hasty temper. 'Light of my eyes, we must get re-married as soon as possible.'

She reminded him that the Law prevented them from marrying again unless another marriage had intervened.

So he called in the aged man who watered the lawn and ordered him to marry her; but it must be a marriage of form only. The obedient gardener did as he was told and, immediately after the ceremony, returned to his watering-pot.

Two days later the woman got run over by a taxi, so the gardener inherited the money and the camels.

I had not realized before just how much the British controlled Egypt. Egypt ranked as an independent kingdom, but it seemed that I owed my principal allegiance not to King Fuad, who had given me my appointment and paid my salary, but to the High Commissioner, whose infantry, cavalry, and air squadrons were a constant reminder of his power. British officials could not understand the Egyptians' desire for independence, considering them most ungrateful for all the beneficent labour and skill applied to their country since the eighties—raising it from bankruptcy to riches. There was no Egyptian nation, I was assured. The Greeks, Turks, Syrians, and Armenians who called themselves Egyptians had no more right there than the British. Before the British occupation the Pashas used to bleed the fellaheen white; and it was not the fellaheen, the only true Egyptians, who now called for freedom. Nationalism, a creed derived from the new smatterings

164

of Western education we were giving the upper classes, should be disregarded as merely a symptom of the country's growing wealth. The reduction of the British official class in the last few years was viewed with disgust. 'We did all the hard work, and when we go everything will run down; it's running down already. And they'll have to call us back, or if not, the dagoes; and we don't see why *they* should benefit.' None of them realized how much the vanity of the Egyptians was hurt by the constant sight of British uniform.

I did two useful pieces of educational work in Egypt. I ordered a consignment of standard text-books of English Literature for the Faculty Library at the University, and I acted as examiner to the diploma class of the Higher Training College which provided English teachers for the primary and secondary schools.

Our children had to drink boiled milk and boiled water, and be constantly watched in case they took off their solar topees and blue veils. Then they all got measles, so were carried off to an isolation hospital and fed on the things that we had been particular since their birth never to give them. They returned thin and wretched-looking—Sam, the baby, with permanently scarred ear-drums—and we wondered if we should ever get them safely back to England. I decided to resign. So did the Professor of Latin, my only English colleague. And the one-legged Professor of French Literature, who was an honest man. The others stayed on.

We booked our passages some time at the end of May, but even after selling the car had only just enough money left to go third-class on a small Italian boat with a cargo of onions. We disembarked at Venice and stopped a day. After Egypt, Venice seemed like Heaven. We ate European eggs there for breakfast. Egyptian eggs were about the size of a pigeon's egg and always tasted strongly of the garlic which seemed to form a large part of the Egyptian fowl's diet.

Egypt gave me plenty of caricature scenes to look back on. For instance: myself wearing a smart yellow gabardine suit and seated at a long, baize-covered table in the Faculty Conference Room. Before me are a cup of Turkish coffee, a solar-topee, and a badly typed French record of the minutes of the last meeting. I am talking angry bad French at my Belgian and French colleagues in support of the young Professor of Latin, who has just leaped to his feet, pale with hatred. He is declaring in worse French that he positively refuses to make a forced contribution of fifty piastres to a memorial wreath for one of the Frenchmen (who had just died), since he was never consulted. I am declaring that neither will I, and that, since the Dean has made a point of excluding us from the previous meetings where he took decisions affecting our lectures, all dead French Professors can go bury themselves at their own expense. It is a lofty, elegant room, once a harem boudoir. A portrait of the late Khedive, with a large rent in it, hangs crookedly at one end; at the other stands a large glass show-case, full of Egypto-Roman bronze coins, muddled together, their labels loose, and the glass cracked. Through the window, market-gardens, buffaloes, camels loaded with green fodder, countrywomen in black. Around the table my horrified, shrugging colleagues, turning to one another and saying: '*Inoui. . . . Inoui. . . .*' And outside the rebellious shouts of our students, working themselves up for another strike.

The rest makes no more than conversation—of the Government clerk who was so doubly unfortunate as to be run over by a racing-car, and then recognize the driver as the eldest son of the Minister of Justice; and of the rich girl in search of a husband, who went as paying guest at fifteen guineas a week to a senior British official's wife, agreeing to pay for all wines and cigars and extras when society came to dine but who, meeting only senior Government officials and their wives, complained that she did not get her money's-worth; and of my night visit to the temple of a headless monkey-god, full of bats; and of the English cotton-manu-facturer who defended conditions in his factory on the ground that the population of Egypt had been increasing far too rapidly under British rule, and that pulmonary consumption remained one of the few checks on it; and of the lame student's mother who, at the sports, said how much she regretted having put him on the mantelpiece when a baby and run off (being only twelve years old) to play with her dolls; and of my visit to Chawki Bey, the national poet of Egypt, in his Moorish mansion by the Nile, who was so like Thomas Hardy, and in whose presence his sons, like good Turks, sat dutifully silent; and of the beggar in the bazaar with too many toes; and of the British colonel who, during the war, on a dream of dearth, had played Joseph, dumping half the wheat of Australia in Egypt, where it found no buyers and was at last eaten by donkeys and camels; and of a visit to ancient dead Heliopolis, with its lovely landscape of green fields, its crooked palm-trees, its water-wheels turned by oxen, and its single obelisk; and of our life in the other Heliopolis, a brand-new dead town on the desert's edge, built by a Belgian company, complete with race-course and Luna Park, where the R.A.F. planes flew low at night among the houses, and where the bored wives of resentful officials wrote novels which they never finished, and painted a little in water colours; and of the little garden of our flat, where I went walking on the first day, among the fruit-trees and flowering shrubs, but came upon no less than eight lean and mangy cats dozing in the beds, and never walked there again. . . .

So back to Islip; much to the disappointment of my parents, who hoped that I had at last seen reason and settled down in a position which equally suited my needs and my talents; and to the undisguised relief of my sister-in-law in Egypt.

The remainder of this story, from 1926 until today, is dramatic but unpublishable. Health and money both improved, marriage wore thin. New characters appeared on the stage. Nancy and I said unforgivable things to each other. We parted on May 6th, 1929. She, of course, insisted on keeping the children. So I went abroad, resolved never to make England my home again; which explains the *Goodbye to All That* of this title.

21

EPILOGUE

THOUGH often asked to publish a continuation of this autobiography, which I wrote in 1929 at the age of thirty-three, I am always glad to report that little of outstanding autobiographical interest has happened since. The proofs of *Goodbye to All That* reached me in Majorca, where I had gone to live as soon as I finished the writing, and which is still my home.

The one serious set-back to my quiet life here came with the Spanish Civil War in 1936, when all British subjects were advised to leave, by warship. I wandered around Europe and the United States for three years; and spent the Second World War in England, because three of my children had joined the Armed Forces—the fourth, Sam, being prevented by deafness from doing the same.

Jenny, my elder daughter, became a W.A.A.F. war-correspondent, entering Paris with General Le Clerc's tanks, and Brussels with General Adair's; and nearly getting killed at Arnhem. Catherine, a W.A.A.F. radio-operator, married Squadron-Leader Clifford Dalton, now Engineer-in-Chief to the Australian Atomic Energy Commission. David joined the First Royal Welch, who had lost very heavily during the defence of Calais, assisted at their famous reunion with the Second Battalion in Madagascar, and then went on with them to India and Burma. He was killed on the Arakan peninsula in March 1943, after going up with a sergeant and one man to bomb the Japanese out of three strong-points, which had held up the battalion's advance. They captured the first strong-point, and when his companions were wounded, David rushed the second single-handed, but was shot through the head trying to take the third. The War Office turned down his recommendation for a posthumous Victoria Cross on the ground that the attack had failed—an Indian battalion retired, the Japanese infiltrated, and what remained of the Royal Welch were forced to cut their way back.

I volunteered for infantry service as soon as war broke out, but when informed that His Majesty could not employ me except in a sedentary appointment, I returned to work—on a book about Sergeant Roger Lamb, who fought with the First Battalion in the American War of 1776–83; and on another about John Milton's behaviour in the English Civil Wars. To avoid getting bombed unnecessarily, I settled in South Devon. Half-way through the war, someone invited me to join the special constabulary, but our village policeman declined to forward my application. His reasons, as I found out by discreet inquiry, were that my German second name made him suspicious; that I had been heard talking a foreign language to two disreputable foreigners—Spanish refugee friends, as it happened, one a major, the other a staff-colonel; and that the words HEIL HITLER! had been found scratched on a vegetable marrow in my garden. So I continued merely as an Air Raid Warden, but took a stern line a few days later when my age-group got called up for medical examination and the policeman brought me a third-class railway-warrant, together with an order to appear before a medical board at Exeter. As an officer on the pensioned list, I refused to travel except first class, a privilege to which my rank entitled me—he and I might find ourselves in the same compartment, and it would never do for us two to mix socially.

Nancy and I eventually got divorced. I married again, have had four more children, enjoy good health, travel as little as possible, and continue to write books. What else can I say, unless that my best friend is still the waste-paper basket? I do not seem to have changed much, mentally or physically, since I came to live here in Majorca, though I can no longer read a newspaper without my glasses, or run upstairs three steps at a time, and have to watch my weight. And if condemned to relive those lost years I should probably behave again in very much the same way.

POEMS BY ROBERT GRAVES

LOST LOVE

His eyes are quickened so with grief,
He can watch a grass or leaf
Every instant grow; he can
Clearly through a flint wall see,
Or watch the startled spirit flee
From the throat of a dead man.

Across two counties he can hear
And catch your words before you speak.
The woodlouse or the maggot's weak
Clamour rings in his sad ear,
And noise so slight it would surpass
Credence—drinking sound of grass,
Worm talk, clashing jaws of moth
Chumbling holes in cloth;
The groan of ants who undertake
Gigantic loads for honour's sake
(their sinews creak, their breath comes thin);
Whir of spiders when they spin,
And minute whispering, mumbling, sighs
Of idle grubs and flies.

This man is quickened so with grief,
He wanders god-like or like thief
Inside and out, below, above,
Without relief seeking lost love.

SYMPTOMS OF LOVE

Love is a universal migraine,
A bright stain on the vision
Blotting out reason.

Symptoms of true love
Are leanness, jealousy,
Laggard dawns;

Are omens and nightmares—
Listening for a knock,
Waiting for a sign:

For a touch of her fingers
In a darkened room,
For a searching look.

Take courage, lover!
Can you endure such grief
At any hand but hers?

WOMAN AND TREE

To love one woman, or to sit
   Always beneath the same tall tree,
Argues a certain lack of wit
   Two steps from imbecility.

A poet, therefore, sworn to feed
   On every food the senses know,
Will claim the inexorable need
   To be Don Juan Tenorio.

Yet if, miraculously enough,
   (And why set miracles apart?)
Woman and tree prove of a stuff
   Wholly to glamour his wild heart?

And if such visions from the void
   As shone in fever there, or there,
Assemble, hold and are enjoyed
   On climbing one familiar stair . . . ?

To change and chance he took a vow,
   As he thought fitting. None the less,
What of a phoenix on the bough,
   Or a sole woman's fatefulness?

THE SECRET LAND

Every woman of true royalty owns
A secret land more real to her
Than this pale outer world:

At midnight when the house falls quiet
She lays aside needle or book
And visits it unseen.

Shutting her eyes, she improvises
A five-barred gate among tall birches,
Vaults over, takes possession.

Then runs, or flies, or mounts a horse
(A horse will canter up to greet her)
And travels where she will;

Can make grass grow, coax lilies up
From bud to blossom as she watches,
Lets fish eat from her palm.

Has founded villages, planted groves
And hollowed valleys for brooks running
Cool to a land-locked bay.

I never dared question my love
About the government of her queendom
Or its geography,

Nor followed her between those birches,
Setting one leg astride the gate,
Spying into the mist.

Yet she has pledged me, when I die,
A lodge beneath her private palace
In a level clearing of the wood
Where gentians grow and gillyflowers
And sometimes we may meet.

ROCKY ACRES

This is a wild land, country of my choice,
With harsh craggy mountain, moor ample and bare.
Seldom in these acres is heard any voice
But voice of cold water that runs here and there
Through rocks and lank heather growing without care.
No mice in the heath run, no song-birds fly
For fear of the buzzard that floats in the sky.

He soars and he hovers, rocking on his wings,
He scans his wide parish with a sharp eye,
He catches the trembling of small hidden things,
He tears them in pieces, dropping them from the sky;
Tenderness and pity the heart will deny,
Where life is but nourished by water and rock—
A hardy adventure, full of fear and shock.

Time has never journeyed to this lost land,
Crakeberry and heather bloom out of date,
The rocks jut, the streams flow singing on either hand,
Careless if the season be early or late,
The skies wander overhead, now blue, now slate;
Winter would be known by his cutting snow
If June did not borrow his armour also.

Yet this is my country, beloved by me best,
The first land that rose from Chaos and the Flood,
Nursing no valleys for comfort or rest,
Trampled by no shod hooves, bought with no blood.
Sempiternal country whose barrows have stood
Stronghold for demigods when on earth they go,
Terror for fat burghers on far plains below.

SPOILS

When all is over and you march for home,
The spoils of war are easily disposed of:
Standards, weapons of combat, helmets, drums
May decorate a staircase or a study,
While lesser gleanings of the battlefield—
Coins, watches, wedding-rings, gold teeth and such—
Are sold anonymously for solid cash.

The spoils of love present a different case,
When all is over and you march for home:
That lock of hair, these letters and the portrait
May not be publicly displayed; nor sold;
Nor burned; nor returned (the heart being obstinate)—
Yet never dare entrust them to a safe
For fear they burn a hole through two-foot steel.

I'M THROUGH WITH YOU FOR EVER

The oddest, surely, of odd tales
   Recorded by the French
Concerns a sneak thief of Marseilles
   Tried by a callous Bench.

His youth, his innocency, his tears—
   No, nothing could abate
Their sentence of 'One hundred years
   In galleys of the State'.

Nevertheless, old wives affirm
   And annalists agree,
He sweated out the whole damned term,
   Bowed stiffly, and went free.

Then come, my angry love, review
   Your sentence of today.
'For ever' was unjust of you,
   The end too far away.

Give me four hundred years, or five—
   Can rage be so intense?—
And I will sweat them out alive
   To prove my impenitence.

FLYING CROOKED

The butterfly, a cabbage-white,
(His honest idiocy of flight)
Will never now, it is too late,
Master the art of flying straight,
Yet has—who knows so well as I?—
A just sense of how not to fly:
He lurches here and here by guess
And God and hope and hopelessness.
Even the aerobatic swift
Has not his flying-crooked gift.

SHE TELLS HER LOVE WHILE HALF ASLEEP

She tells her love while half asleep,
   In the dark hours,
     With half-words whispered low:
As Earth stirs in her winter sleep
   And puts out grass and flowers
     Despite the snow,
     Despite the falling snow.

BROTHER

It's odd enough to be alive with others,
But odder still to have sisters and brothers:
To make one of a characteristic litter—
The sisters puzzled and vexed, the brothers vexed and bitter
That this one wears, though flattened by abuse,
The family nose for individual use.